EUROPEAN DESSERTS
FOR AMERICAN KITCHENS

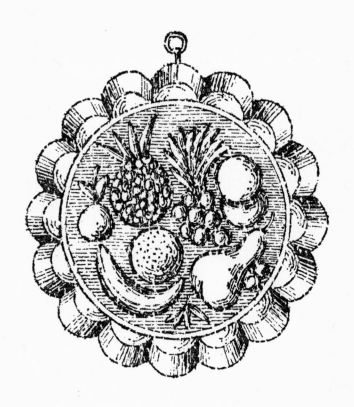

EUROPEAN DESSERTS
FOR
AMERICAN KITCHENS

By Elaine Ross

With drawings by John Alcorn

HASTINGS HOUSE PUBLISHERS • NEW YORK 22

CONTENTS

INTRODUCTION

When the show window of a *pâtisserie* rivals a neighboring jewelry display to hold a woman's gaze, it's dollars to doughnuts, or should I say diamonds to *Dobosch Torten*, that master bakers are at work here.

From recent trips to Europe I can report only in general on the fashion scene, but I can describe in minutia the violet-studded pyramid of whipped cream arabesques that crowned an iced *soufflé* I ate in Paris and I can almost taste a subtly-flavored pudding I enjoyed so much in Lisbon not too long ago.

Though my interest in these matters exceeds the norm (since food, to me, is of professional preoccupation), I am not alone in my enthusiasm for delicacies seen and tasted in Europe. How many a returning tourist launches a personal travelogue in gustatory hyperbole!

My travels have led, by intent, to many a gastronomic mecca, and, by chance, to any number of obscure hostelries and shops where I have applauded the efforts of still unrecognized geniuses. And one thing was true throughout: A request for a recipe, a query regarding a culinary procedure was graciously answered—sometimes, of necessity, in sign language, though cooks seem to have an Esperanto all their own. On my return home each recipe, often no more than a series of notes, was tested, adjusted, and added to my files. From these I have chosen a representation, geographical and categorical, of European desserts.

Why desserts? Perhaps my overactive sweet tooth dictated the choice, although I rather think there is also a practical reason. More than any other component of a meal, desserts are suitable for more than one occasion. The same yeast cake that teams so fragrantly with morning coffee, will complement the afternoon tea table equally well. Yeast cake is a fitting finale to a simple meal, or it might be the focal point of a late evening snack. Or consider pancakes: Creamy cheese-filled *crêpes* that are served after a light supper are superb as a main course at luncheon. Fruit desserts are often the perfect foil for a poultry dish on a buffet table. Climax an elegant dinner party with an exquisite many-layered *torte*, or feature it in splendor when you invite friends in for dessert and coffee.

And why just European desserts? Obviously, my feeling that there is a need for such a collection, arises from the unprecedented number of sorties of Americans to Europe during these past years. The returning traveler has a new concept of food, an awareness of the *art* of cooking, an appreciation of dining leisurely and graciously, and a desire to follow suit. The sale of imported delicacies and the publication of more and more foreign recipes bear this out.

I assembled this collection thoughtfully. It was not to be vast, for then it must of necessity be encyclopedic. It is intended rather to be choice; to offer a taste of many countries, a sampling of the greats of culinary tradition as well as a host of little-known recipes. I talked with eminent chefs in their kitchens and I chatted with housewives on park benches and in marketplaces. From both, I learned.

The contents of this book are not all-inclusive, nor is the general advice and counsel on cooking method and procedure. Such material is well-covered in standard texts. What I have to say is not always basic, but I trust it will be helpful. These things I have learned in my kitchen.

I hope your equipment includes an electric mixer, and I have assumed so in giving the recipe directions. Even the small portable type will help to save your strength and temper, and to underwrite a smooth and fluffy batter. This does not mean that you *cannot* get along without one; it's just a question of conserving energy and time. Indeed, many a great chef would not dream of using an electric beater. He relies on his whisk and his wrist to produce the lightest batter and the airiest meringue.

I, too, am devoted to my whisks, but for quite another purpose. To guarantee a sauce or *crème pâtissière* absolutely free of lumps, there is nothing to equal a whisk. I use two kinds; the standard French wire whisk, and the Scandinavian whisk. The latter, which consists of a bunch of fine twigs tied together, I use mainly when I work in a metal pot or bowl. Here I do not like to use the wire whisk because I feel that metal on metal produces infinitesimal scrapings that affect the taste.

Throughout this book there are many recipes using ground nuts. Do not grind them in a meat grinder, or they will come out mashed and pasty. Use either an electric blender or a grinder specifically designed for nuts. Some meat grinders have special nut attachments. It is a matter of minutes to grind a pound of nuts, put them in a covered jar, and store them in the refrigerator where they keep almost indefinitely. (In many large cities you can buy freshly ground nuts in specialty stores.) In following these recipes do not pack the ground nuts into a measuring cup. Spoon them in lightly. The amounts given for nuts before grinding, refer to shelled, unblanched nutmeats, unless otherwise specified.

I use my blender or nut grinder to make bread and cooky crumbs. In Europe I learned to use fine bread crumbs rather than flour to dust a greased pan. Since then, I have rarely had trouble getting a cake out of a pan. If I do, my first-aid tool is a very fine steel knitting needle; it gets into little corners that a knife can't get to.

I have solved my other *sticking* problem too. Some cookies, particularly lacy wafers, must remain on the baking sheet to stiffen for a minute or two after being removed from the oven. If you do not remove them quickly enough then, they become too brittle. Directions often specify replacing them in the oven for a few seconds, but I find it better to place the baking sheet over low heat on top of the stove. With a spatula, remove the cookies from the heated area; they loosen immediately without getting too soft again. This same trick works for the bottom of a stubborn cake, too.

I have invested in some of the lovely French scalloped tart tins, both large and small. They enhance the appearance of the finished tart by giving it a professional look. (These are generally available in well-stocked housewares departments. If you don't have one nearby, it is possible to order them by mail.) To remove the sides of the tin, place the cooled baked tart on a tin can (a coffee tin is just right), and the sides will drop to the countertop.

My tins range from one to twelve inches in diameter. When I use the smaller ones I place them on a baking sheet to go into the oven. It's much easier and safer than putting them on the oven shelf one by one. Some tins have very tiny scalloped sides. To grease them thoroughly, melt the shortening, and apply it with a pastry brush; you won't miss any spots this way.

When a recipe calls for a prebaked shell into which fruit or filling is spooned, and the weather is damp and humid, you can avoid soggy shells by waiting until just before servingtime to add the filling. Where fillings are baked in a raw crust, set the tin on the bottom shelf of the oven to ensure thorough baking of the bottom crust.

To roll out a rich tart dough for a large tart, place the dough between two sheets of waxed paper, roll out the dough, peel off the top paper, invert the pastry into the tin, and carefully remove the remaining paper. To line tiny tins with the dough, press the dough into the tins with your thumbs, lightly floured.

When it comes to cakes, there is little I have to add to what has already been said in other sources. A purchase that has repaid me manifold in time saved was an extra set of beaters for the electric mixer. I don't have to stop to wash the beaters after beating a batter and before beating the egg whites; instead, I pop in the spare set. If you have just one set, separate the eggs first, reserve the yolks in a cup until they are needed, and beat the whites stiff *before* you beat the rest of the cake batter. (Working in this order, you need not wash the beaters.)

Where spices are called for in a cake or any other recipe, you may assume that they are powdered. Nutmeg, ginger, etc., are generally sold in powdered form, so it did not seem necessary to specify "powdered" in the recipe. Since cardamom and cloves *are* sold whole as often as powdered, I did specify which one of these was needed.

When I bake a large batch of cake or cookies that necessitates using two shelves in the oven, I shift the position of the cake or cookies toward the end of the baking time, to ensure even baking. Baking a full oven load generally requires slightly longer baking time.

To frost a cake on a serving platter without messing the platter, place four 2-inch-wide strips of waxed paper under the bottom edges of the cake. Proceed with the frosting, gently pull out the paper, and the platter is left spotless. To produce a whipped cream with good body for frosting, chill the bowl, the beaters, and the cream.

Save left-over cake that is past its prime in the freezer; slice it, and substitute it for ladyfingers in an icebox cake. Often the left-over frosting can be added to the icebox cake filling with interesting results.

When you improvise either an icebox-cake filling or a chilled pudding calling for gelatine, and you are not sure how much gelatine to use, a general rule of thumb is 1 tablespoon of gelatine to 2 cups of liquid. However, if you use a substantial amount of cake between the layers of filling, or if you use a fruit purée or custard that is not completely liquid as part of your filling, you may be puzzled. Most certainly you want your cake or pudding to hold up, but you do not want it so solid as to appear indestructible. If you are not sure, add half a tablespoon of dissolved gelatine for each 2 cups of filling, pour a spoonful of the filling into a cup, set it in the freezer for a few minutes, and you will have your answer. If it has set, you know that you have enough; if not, add a bit more dissolved gelatine and try again.

A freezer permits advance preparation of *soufflés* and *crêpes* filled or covered with a *soufflé* mixture. This is a lifesaver when you have guests. As far ahead as an hour and a half before servingtime, prepare the *soufflé* or the *crêpes* ready for baking, and store in the freezer until 10 minutes before bakingtime. Leave at room temperature for 10 minutes; if you put the dish directly into a hot oven, it might crack. In these recipes, the baking time is gauged to produce a moist *soufflé;* if you prefer a dry *soufflé*, add a few minutes.

I find it a great help to keep a stockpile of ready-to-use *crêpes* in my freezer. Pack a stack of 12 *crêpes* in freezer-weight foil, and freeze. To defrost them, preheat the oven to 350°, and place the foil package in the oven until the *crêpes* are defrosted.

I keep a goodly inventory of cookies and small cakes in the freezer. You will notice more recipes in these categories than in any other, simply because I feel they are so useful. Cookies defrost in a few minutes; small cakes take a little longer. Serve them with fruits or ice cream for dessert, arrange a pretty assortment for the tea tray, or add a platter of cookies and cakes to a buffet table. And, no matter how small the freezer, it will house an amazing quantity of cookies.

I usually make yeast cakes in large quantities, half to be served immediately, half for the freezer. They freeze beautifully, and can be defrosted in the oven. Since I feel that yeast cake is at its best slightly warm, defrosting in the oven is all to the good. Why so many people are afraid to tackle yeast dough I cannot understand. It thrives on vigorous beating and rough kneading. Two things to remember: Do not use yeast that has passed the expiration date stamped on the package, and make certain that the yeast is thoroughly dissolved before you incorporate it into the dough.

In gathering the material for this book, I have struck only one bone of contention, and that, an amusing one. Disagreements on the ingredients of a recipe or cooking methods were rare and of minor consequence. But assign a recipe to a country of origin, and the fur flies! Everyone wants the honor of having thought of it first. How many yellow-paged cookbooks, how many faded, handwritten recipes were put forth as proof positive that a given recipe was of a certain origin. As you travel from one European country to the next, you inevitably discover the counterpart of almost all recipes in each country. A nuance is changed here or there, but essentially they are the same. And so, gradually, this became the *one* area in which I studiously avoided asking questions! Perhaps everyone has a fair claim. I really think it most likely, and on this assumption, I have put down these recipes.

ELAINE ROSS

CAKES

LIGHT CAKES

Blitzkuchen (Lightning Cake)

Prinsesstårta (Marzipan-Frosted Layer Cake)

Spongecake Natasha

Roule aux Marrons (Marron Roll)

Tartan Tea Cake

Mrs. Bertelsen's Norwegian Tosca Cake

Dame Pettycock's Trifle Cake

Szegedin Cake (Filled Coffee Cake)

Rum Cake Stresa

Pound Cake (See Whiskey Seed Pound Cake, page 21)

Jelly Roll (see Charlotte Russe, page 212)

Blitzkuchen (Lightning Cake)

Blitz is indeed accurate; this cake is made as fast as lightning. Moist and finely-textured, it goes well with afternoon tea or coffee, or as dessert for a simple meal.

Preheat oven to 375°. Cream ¼ pound butter with 1 cup sugar until light and fluffy. Separate 4 eggs. Reserve 1 white for topping. Beat in 4 egg yolks and 2 teaspoons grated lemon rind. Sift 1 cup plus 2 tablespoons flour with 1 teaspoon baking powder, and fold into batter alternately with 3 tablespoons milk. Beat 3 egg whites until stiff but not dry, fold into batter, and spread in a greased 9-by-12-inch pan.

Dilute the reserved egg white with 1 tablespoon water, and spread over batter. Mix ¾ cup sugar, 2 teaspoons cinnamon, and ½ cup finely chopped walnuts, sprinkle over batter, and bake for 25 minutes, or until cake starts to shrink from sides of pan. Cool cake in pan, and cut into 12 rectangles.

¼ pound butter	3 tablespoons milk
1 cup sugar	1 tablespoon water
4 eggs	¾ cup sugar
2 teaspoons grated lemon rind	2 teaspoons cinnamon
1 cup plus 2 tablespoons flour	½ cup finely chopped walnuts
1 teaspoon baking powder	

YIELD: 12 servings

Prinsesstårta (Marzipan-Frosted Layer Cake)

Preheat oven to 350°. Beat 3 eggs with ¾ cup sugar until thick and light. Sift together 6 tablespoons flour, 6 tablespoons potato flour, and ¾ teaspoon baking powder. Fold into egg-sugar mixture, and pour into 2 greased and floured 9-inch layer-cake

3

pans. Bake for 25 minutes, or until top of cake springs back when pressed lightly. Remove from oven, and turn out onto racks to cool.

While the layers are baking, make ½ recipe *Crème Pâtissière* (see Index). Cool, then fold in ½ cup heavy cream, whipped until stiff. Grind ¾ cup blanched almonds, using the finest blade of the meat grinder. Add ¾ cup confectioners' sugar, and grind again. With your fingers, work in as much of 1 egg white as is necessary to bring the paste to a dough-like consistency that can be rolled out. Place the nut paste between 2 large sheets of waxed paper, and roll out into a circle large enough to cover the top and sides of cake.

Spread one layer with half of the cream filling, place the second layer on top, and spread with the remaining filling. Loosen paper from almond paste. Place a rolling pin on center of paste, carefully fold paste in half over pin, lift sheet of paste, and place on top of cake. Gently press the paste around sides of cake, and trim around bottom edge. Dust top with confectioners' sugar, and refrigerate until servingtime.

3 eggs	½ cup heavy cream
¾ cup sugar	¾ cup blanched almonds
6 tablespoons flour	¾ cup confectioners' sugar
6 tablespoons potato flour	1 egg white
¾ teaspoon baking powder	
½ recipe *Crème Pâtissière* (see Index)	

YIELD: 10 servings

Spongecake Natasha

Preheat oven to 325°. Beat 6 egg yolks with 1 cup sugar until thick and light. Fold in ¾ cup cake flour, sifted, and the grated rind of 1 lemon. Fold in 6 egg whites, beaten until very stiff. Working quickly, fold in ¼ cup sour cream, pour into an ungreased 9-inch tube pan, and bake for 50 minutes, or until the top springs back when pressed lightly. (You must do the last step quickly, or the fat in the sour cream will break down the stability of the beaten whites.) Invert the pan on a cake rack, and let cake cool completely before removing it from the pan. Dust the top generously with confectioners' sugar.

6 egg yolks	6 egg whites
1 cup sugar	¼ cup sour cream
¾ cup cake flour	Confectioners' sugar
Grated rind of 1 lemon	

YIELD: 8 servings

Roule aux Marrons (Marron Roll)

Preheat oven to 350°. Grease a 10-by-15-inch jelly-roll pan, line with waxed paper, and grease the paper thoroughly. Beat 5 egg whites until stiff but not dry. In a separate bowl, beat 5 egg yolks with ⅓ cup sugar until thick and light. Beat in 3 tablespoons flour, sifted, fold in the beaten whites, and spread batter in prepared pan. Bake for 15 minutes, invert on a piece of waxed paper, and peel off top paper. Starting from the short side, roll up the cake, and cool.

While the cake is cooling, drain 12 marrons, preserved in syrup. Chop coarsely, and sprinkle with 1 tablespoon cognac. Whip 2 cups of heavy cream until stiff with ¼ cup Vanilla Sugar (see Index). When the cake is cool, unroll, and sprinkle with 1 tablespoon cognac. Fold the marrons into half the cream, spread on the cake, and reroll. Place on serving platter, and frost with remaining cream.

This is an excellent basic roll that lends itself to a variety of fillings: Whipped cream with diced fresh fruit; drained, preserved, or brandied fruit; coarsely grated chocolate; Chocolate Butter Cream (see Index); or *Crème Pâtissière* (see Index).

5 egg whites	1 tablespoon cognac
5 egg yolks	2 cups heavy cream
⅓ cup sugar	¼ cup Vanilla Sugar (see Index)
3 tablespoons flour	1 tablespoon cognac
12 marrons, preserved in syrup	YIELD: 8 to 10 servings

Tartan Tea Cake

A cake of this *genre* should be in every baking repertoire. It is quick and easy to make and has a moist and tender texture without being overly rich. It is excellent served with no more than a dusting of confectioners' sugar, or, bake it in two 9-inch layers for 25 to 30 minutes, and go to town on filling and frosting. Almost as fast as making a cake from a prepared mix, and so much better!

Preheat oven to 375°. Cream ¼ pound butter with 1½ cups sugar until light and fluffy. Beat in 3 eggs, one at a time, beating well after each addition. Sift 2 cups flour with 2 teaspoons baking powder, and add to the batter alternately with ½ cup milk. Add 1 teaspoon vanilla and ½ teaspoon almond extract, and pour into a well-greased 9-inch tube pan. Bake for 40 to 45 minutes, or until a cake tester, inserted in the center of the cake, comes out clean. Turn out onto a cake rack and cool. Dust with confectioners' sugar.

¼ pound butter	½ cup milk
1½ cups sugar	1 teaspoon vanilla
3 eggs	½ teaspoon almond extract
2 cups flour	Confectioners' sugar
2 teaspoons baking powder	YIELD: 8 to 10 servings

Mrs. Bertelsen's Norwegian Tosca Cake

Preheat oven to 350°. Melt ¼ pound butter, and cool completely. Beat 3 eggs with ½ cup sugar until very thick and light. Fold in ½ cup flour, sifted; then, very slowly, fold in the butter. Pour into a greased 9-inch layer-cake pan, and bake for 25 minutes. Remove cake from oven, spread with topping, below, and replace in oven for 5 minutes more.

To make the topping, place in a saucepan: 5 tablespoons each butter and sugar, ⅔ cup sliced blanched almonds, 1 teaspoon flour, and 1 tablespoon milk. Just before the cake has finished baking, cook, stirring constantly, for 3 or 4 minutes until honey-colored.

¼ pound butter	5 tablespoons sugar
3 eggs	⅔ cup sliced blanched almonds
½ cup sugar	1 teaspoon flour
½ cup flour	1 tablespoon milk
5 tablespoons butter	

YIELD: 6 servings

Dame Pettycock's Trifle Cake

This recipe was given to me by a sprightly English lady who managed to break with tradition, and dreamed up this departure from the classic English Trifle. Should you prefer to adhere to the time-honored version, substitute 16 ladyfingers or pieces of spongecake, purchased or home-made. Sprinkle the cake with a little brandy and sherry, and place in a deep dish. Cover the cake with almond macaroons, dot with jam, pour over the custard, and spread cream on top. Essentially the two recipes are the same; it's mainly a question of presentation.

Preheat oven to 350°. Melt 1 tablespoon butter, and cool. Beat 3 eggs with 3 tablespoons sugar until thick and light. Fold in ¼ cup flour, then fold in the butter. Pour into a greased 9-inch layer-cake pan, and bake for 20 to 25 minutes, or until the top springs back when pressed lightly. Turn out onto a cake rack, and cool.

While the cake is baking, make the custard: In a saucepan, with a whisk, beat 4 eggs, 3 tablespoons sugar, and 2 teaspoons cornstarch. Gradually add 2 cups milk. Cook, over low heat, stirring constantly, until thick. Remove from heat, add 1 teaspoon of vanilla, and cool.

Place the cake on a serving platter, and spread the custard on top (don't worry if some runs down the sides). Dot with 3 tablespoons of softened raspberry or currant jelly, and cover with 1 pound of almond macaroons, crumbled. Whip 1 cup of heavy cream until stiff, spread over the macaroons, and chill.

1 tablespoon butter	2 cups milk
3 eggs	1 teaspoon vanilla
3 tablespoons sugar	3 tablespoons softened rasp-
¼ cup flour	berry or currant jelly
4 eggs	1 pound almond macaroons
3 tablespoons sugar	1 cup heavy cream
2 teaspoons cornstarch	

YIELD: 10 servings

Szegedin Cake (Filled Coffee Cake)

In a small bowl, place ½ cup flour, ¼ teaspoon baking powder, 1 tablespoon cinnamon, ¾ cup brown sugar, 2 tablespoons very soft butter, and ¼ cup finely chopped walnuts. With your fingertips, mix all ingredients until they form crumbs.

Preheat oven to 375°. Cream ¼ pound butter, ¼ cup vegetable shortening, and 1 cup sugar until light and fluffy. Beat in 3 egg yolks. Sift together 3 cups flour, 1 teaspoon salt, and 4 teaspoons baking powder. Add to the batter alternately with 1 cup sour cream and 1 teaspoon vanilla. Beat 3 egg whites until stiff but not dry, and fold in. Pour half the batter into a greased 10-inch tube pan, and sprinkle with half the crumbs. Cover with 1 large apple, peeled and thinly sliced, and dot with 2 tablespoons currant jelly. Pour in the remaining batter, sprinkle with the remaining crumbs, and bake for 1 hour, or until a cake tester inserted in the center of the cake comes out clean. Turn out onto a cake rack to cool.

½ cup flour	3 egg yolks
¼ teaspoon baking powder	3 cups flour
1 tablespoon cinnamon	1 teaspoon salt
¾ cup brown sugar	4 teaspoons baking powder
2 tablespoons butter	1 cup sour cream
¼ cup finely chopped walnuts	1 teaspoon vanilla
¼ pound butter	3 egg whites
¼ cup vegetable shortening	1 large apple
1 cup sugar	2 tablespoons currant jelly

YIELD: 12 servings

Rum Cake Stresa

Preheat oven to 325°. Grease an 8-inch fluted tube pan very generously, and dust with 2 tablespoons fine dry bread crumbs. Beat 3 egg whites until foamy, add ½ teaspoon cream of tartar, and 2 tablespoons sugar, continuing to beat until stiff. Beat 3 egg yolks with ¼ cup sugar until thick and light. Stir in ½ teaspoon almond extract and 2 tablespoons currants. Sift ½ cup cake flour with ½ teaspoon baking powder, and fold into the egg-yolk mixture alternately with the beaten whites. Pour into prepared pan, and bake for 35 to 40 minutes, or until top springs back when pressed lightly. Turn out onto a plate.

Make a rum syrup by bringing ¼ cup sugar and ½ cup water to a rolling boil. Remove from heat, and add ¼ cup light rum and ½ teaspoon almond extract. Pour rum syrup over cake and cool. In a small saucepan, over low heat, melt 2 ounces semisweet chocolate in 2 tablespoons coffee, and spread over cooled cake.

2 tablespoons fine dry bread crumbs
3 egg whites
½ teaspoon cream of tartar
2 tablespoons sugar
3 egg yolks
¼ cup sugar
½ teaspoon almond extract
2 tablespoons currants

½ cup cake flour
½ teaspoon baking powder
¼ cup sugar
½ cup water
¼ cup light rum
½ teaspoon almond extract
2 ounces semisweet chocolate
2 tablespoons coffee

YIELD: 6 servings

CHOCOLATE CAKES

---•◆•---

Prinz Pückler Cake (A German Chocolate Cake)

Bernese Chocolate Cake

Bûche aux Marrons (Chocolate Roll with Marron Filling)

Bûche aux Pistaches (Chocolate Roll with Pistachio Filling—
see *Bûche aux Marrons*)

Chocolade Koek (Dutch Chocolate Cake)

Gâteau de Chocolat aux Cerises (Chocolate Cherry Cake)

Dos Caballeros (Date Chocolate Cake)

Chocolate Sandwich Cake

Prinz Pückler Cake (A German Chocolate Cake)

Preheat oven to 375°. In the top of a double boiler, melt 4 ounces semisweet chocolate. Cream ¼ pound butter with 6 egg yolks. Add ½ cup sugar and the melted chocolate, continuing to beat rapidly. Beat 6 egg whites until stiff but not dry, and fold into the batter. Lastly, fold in 1 cup sifted cake flour. Pour mixture into 3 greased and floured 9-inch layer-cake pans, and bake for 17 minutes, or until a cake tester inserted in the center of the cake comes out clean. (It is unusual to fold in the flour after the stiffly beaten egg whites, but if you add the flour first, the batter is very heavy and will break down the beaten whites.) Turn out layers on cake racks, and cool.

While the layers are baking, make the filling: Soak 2 teaspoons gelatine in 2 tablespoons cold water. In a saucepan, mix 7 egg yolks with ⅓ cup sugar. Gradually add 1 cup milk. Cook over low heat, stirring constantly until thick. Do not allow to boil. Remove from heat, stir in the soaked gelatine, and cool for 15 minutes. Beat in 7 ounces of sweet butter and 2 tablespoons rum, then fold in ⅓ cup diced, candied citron or other candied fruit. Chill until firm enough to spread. Spread filling between the layers, and frost the top and sides of cake with ½ recipe Chocolate Frosting #3 (see Index). Garnish with halved, candied cherries.

4 ounces semisweet chocolate	⅓ cup sugar
¼ pound butter	1 cup milk
6 egg yolks	7 ounces sweet butter
½ cup sugar	2 tablespoons rum
6 egg whites	⅓ cup diced, candied citron or
1 cup sifted cake flour	other candied fruit
2 teaspoons gelatine	½ recipe Chocolate Frosting #3
2 tablespoons cold water	(see Index)
7 egg yolks	Halved, candied cherries

YIELD: 12 to 16 servings

Bernese Chocolate Cake

Preheat oven to 350°. In the top of a double boiler, melt 2½ ounces semisweet chocolate. Cream 5 tablespoons butter with ⅓ cup sugar until light and fluffy. Beat in 1½ eggs, reserving the extra ½ egg. (To divide a whole egg, beat it lightly with a fork; once the yolk and white are blended, it's easy to take a portion of it.) Add the melted chocolate and 5 tablespoons light corn syrup, and continue beating. Sift 1 cup flour with 1 teaspoon baking powder, and add to the batter alternately with 6 tablespoons sour cream. Pour into a well-greased 8-inch-square tin, and bake for 25 minutes, or until cake tester comes out clean. Turn cake out onto a cake rack, and cool.

While the cake is baking, prepare a butter cream filling: In the small bowl of the electric mixer, place 1 cup confectioners' sugar, 5 tablespoons sweet butter, 1 egg yolk, and 2½ table-spoons cocoa. Beat until light and fluffy.

Also prepare almond paste: In a small bowl, using your hands, blend ½ cup each ground almonds and confectioners' sugar with as much of the reserved ½ egg as it takes to hold the mixture together, and make it just pasty enough so that you can roll it out with a rolling pin. Add the egg very gradually; the mixture must not be too sticky. Place the almond paste be-tween 2 pieces of waxed paper, roll out to an 8½-inch square, and trim edges.

Split the cooled cake into 2 layers, spread the bottom layer with butter cream, and replace top layer. Peel the top piece of waxed paper from the almond paste. Holding the other piece of waxed paper, invert onto top of cake. (The waxed paper is now on top.) Gently peel off this paper.

Prepare ½ recipe Chocolate Frosting #3 (see Index), and immediately spread over top of cake.

This may sound like a lot of work for one cake; though it is true that the recipe has four component parts, each is relatively quick, and the net result is excellent. You may substitute ⅓ cup of commercially prepared almond paste; if necessary, thin it with a little cream.

2½ ounces semisweet chocolate	5 tablespoons sweet butter
5 tablespoons butter	1 egg yolk
⅓ cup sugar	2½ tablespoons cocoa
1½ eggs	½ cup ground almonds
5 tablespoons light corn syrup	½ cup confectioners' sugar
1 cup flour	½ egg
1 teaspoon baking powder	½ recipe Chocolate Frosting #3
6 tablespoons sour cream	(see Index)
1 cup confectioners' sugar	

YIELD: 8 servings

Bûche aux Marrons

A variation on the Christmas *bûche,* and a handsome and delicious log it is. If chestunts are not your choice, make a *Bûche aux Pistaches:* Instead of the chestnut filling and frosting, whip 2 cups heavy cream until stiff with ⅓ cup Vanilla Sugar (see Index), and divide into 2 bowls. To one bowl, add 4 candied cherries, minced, and ¼ cup chopped pistachio nuts. Spread on the cake, roll up, and frost the outside with the plain whipped cream. With additional candied cherries, cut in half or quarters, and slender strips of angelica, make a few Christmas flowers on top.

Preheat oven to 375°. Grease a 10-by-15-inch jelly-roll pan, line with waxed paper, and grease the paper thoroughly. In the large bowl of the electric mixer, beat 5 eggs with ½ cup confectioners' sugar for 10 to 15 minutes until thick and light. Lightly fold in ⅓ cup sifted cocoa, and 1 teaspoon vanilla. Pour into prepared pan, and bake for 12 to 13 minutes, or until the cake just starts to shrink from the sides of the pan. Sprinkle cake generously with confectioners' sugar, place a piece of waxed paper on top, and invert the cake on a board. Working quickly, peel off the top piece of waxed paper (that originally lined the pan), and, starting from the narrow side, roll up the cake, and cool.

Cream ¼ pound sweet butter with ¼ cup confectioners' sugar. Add the contents of a 1-pound can of sweetened, puréed chestnuts (available at delicacy or fine food shops), and ¼ cup kirsch.

Unroll the cake, spread with half the filling, roll up, and spread the *bûche* with remaining filling. Score with the tines of a fork to simulate a bark-like texture, and garnish with crystallized violets.

5 eggs	¼ cup confectioners' sugar
½ cup confectioners' sugar	1-pound can of sweetened
⅓ cup sifted cocoa	puréed chestnuts
1 teaspoon vanilla	¼ cup kirsch
Confectioners' sugar	Crystallized violets
¼ pound sweet butter	

YIELD: 8 to 10 servings

Chocolade Koek (Dutch Chocolate Cake)

I ate this cake in a private home in Amsterdam. My hostess was kind enough to give me the recipe; I've never seen another quite like it.

Preheat oven to 350°. In a small saucepan, stirring constantly, over low heat, melt 6 ounces dark sweet chocolate in 3 tablespoons strong coffee. Remove from heat, add 1 tablespoon Curacao, and set aside for a few minutes.

Beat 6 egg yolks with ⅔ cup sugar until thick and light. Fold in chocolate and 6 stiffly beaten egg whites. Pour ⅔ of the batter into a greased 9-inch spring-form pan and bake for 25 minutes. Turn off heat, and leave cake in the oven 5 minutes longer. (When you put the cake in the oven, place the remaining batter in the refrigerator.) Let the cake cool in the pan for 1½ hours, during which time the center of the cake will settle, and the edges will remain high, forming a rim. Run a sharp knife around the inside of the pan to loosen the cake, and remove the sides of the pan. Carefully, spread the chilled, uncooked batter over the top of the cake, excluding the rim, and place the cake in the refrigerator for 2 hours. With a sharp knife, loosen the cake from the bottom of the pan, and slide cake onto a serving platter. Whip ⅓ cup heavy cream until stiff with 1 tablespoon sugar. Spoon into a pastry tube fitted with a star-shaped opening, and press out the cream in small rosettes to cover the rim of the cake. Sprinkle 1 tablespoon grated chocolate on the center of the cake.

6 ounces dark sweet chocolate	6 egg whites
3 tablespoons strong coffee	⅓ cup heavy cream
1 tablespoon Curacao	1 tablespoon sugar
6 egg yolks	1 tablespoon grated chocolate
⅔ cup sugar	YIELD: 6 to 8 servings

Gâteau de Chocolat aux Cerises (Cherry Chocolate Cake)

Preheat oven to 350°. Drain a 1-pound can of pitted sour cherries in syrup. In the top of a double boiler, melt ½ cup chocolate bits. Cream ¾ cup butter with ⅔ cup sugar until light and fluffy. Add 3 eggs, one at a time, beating well after each addition. Add the melted chocolate, ⅔ cup ground almonds, and ⅔ cup flour sifted with 1 teaspoon baking powder. Beat only until blended, and pour into a greased 8-inch spring-form pan. Place the cherries evenly on top of the batter, and bake for 1 hour, or until the cake starts to shrink from the sides of the pan.

Cool the cake in the pan, remove cake to a board, and frost the sides only with ½ recipe Chocolate Frosting #3 (see Index), reserving a little frosting to dribble on top. When frosting is set, remove the cake to a serving platter.

1 1-pound can of pitted sour cherries in syrup	⅔ cup ground almonds
½ cup chocolate bits	⅔ cup flour
¾ cup butter	1 teaspoon baking powder
⅔ cup sugar	½ recipe Chocolate Frosting #3 (see Index)
3 eggs	

YIELD: 8 servings

Dos Caballeros (Date Chocolate Cake)

My informant swears that this is the gospel truth. According to family legend, when her grandmother was very young, there was a cook at home who made a fantastic chocolate cake that never managed to arrive intact at the dinner table. When her grandmother and her sisters and brothers were questioned, there was always a wide-eyed explanation involving two *caballeros,* swords and guns and dire threats if at least a portion of the treasure wasn't handed over forthwith.

Preheat oven to 350°. Put ½ cup pitted dates, packed, through the meat grinder, using the coarse blade. Sprinkle ⅓ teaspoon baking soda over the dates, pour ¼ cup hot water over them, and set aside. In the top of a double boiler, melt 1 ounce each semisweet and bitter chocolate. Cream ¼ pound butter with ⅔ cup sugar until light and fluffy. Beat in 1 egg, the melted chocolate, ½ teaspoon vanilla, and the reserved dates with their liquid. Mix ¾ cup flour with ¼ teaspoon salt, and add to the batter alternately with ⅓ cup sour cream. Pour into a well-greased 8-inch-square pan, and bake for 45 minutes. Turn out of pan onto a cake rack to cool.

Mix 6 tablespoons confectioners' sugar with 1 tablespoon cocoa. Add 2 teaspoons brandy, stir until smooth, and dribble in a lacy pattern over the cooled cake.

½ cup pitted dates, packed	½ teaspoon vanilla
⅛ teaspoon baking soda	¾ cup flour
¼ cup hot water	¼ teaspoon salt
1 ounce semisweet chocolate	⅓ cup sour cream
1 ounce bitter chocolate	6 tablespoons confectioners'
¼ pound butter	sugar
⅔ cup sugar	1 tablespoon cocoa
1 egg	2 teaspoons brandy

YIELD: 6 to 8 servings

Chocolate Sandwich Cake

Preheat oven to 350°. In a small saucepan, over low heat, stirring constantly, melt 2 ounces of semisweet chocolate and 1½ ounces of bitter chocolate in 6½ tablespoons of water. In a mixing bowl, cream ½ pound sweet butter with 1½ cups sugar until light and fluffy. Add 3 eggs, 2 egg yolks, and the melted chocolate, and beat thoroughly. Sift 2 cups cake flour with 1 teaspoon soda and ⅔ teaspoon salt, and add to the batter alternately with ¾ cup sour cream and 1½ teaspoons vanilla. Beat until well blended, pour into 3 well-greased 8-inch layer cake pans, and bake for 35 minutes, or until the cake just starts to shrink from the sides of the pans. Turn out onto a cake rack to cool.

While the cake is baking, prepare Chocolate Butter Cream (see Index). Spread the butter cream thickly between the cooled layers and on top of the cake, reserving a little of the cream. Spoon the reserved cream into a pastry tube fitted with a star-shaped opening, and force out in rosettes around the circumference of the cake.

2 ounces semisweet chocolate	2 cups cake flour
1½ ounces bitter chocolate	1 teaspoon soda
6½ tablespoons water	⅔ teaspoon salt
½ pound sweet butter	¾ cup sour cream
1½ cups sugar	1½ teaspoons vanilla
3 eggs	1 recipe Chocolate Butter
2 egg yolks	Cream (see Index)

YIELD: 12 servings

FRUIT AND NUT CAKES

Whiskey Seed Pound Cake

Andalusia (Kirsch Nut Ring)

Light Fruit Cake (see Whiskey Seed Pound Cake)

Simnel Cake (Almond Paste Fruit Cake)

Scotch Black Bun (Fruit Cake in a Crust)

Cake of the *Bodega* (Orange Nut Cake)

Fröken Dohrman's Apple Cake

Bischofsbrot (Chocolate-Studded Fruit and Nut Loaf)

Cottage Cheese *Stollen*

Pain de Gênes (Almond Cake)

Whiskey Seed Pound Cake

Though the addition of caraway seeds and candied peel will not improve a fine pound cake, it will produce a new and subtle off-beat flavor. Use this basic recipe, without peel and seeds, for traditional Pound Cake, or stud the batter generously with dried fruits, candied peels, and nuts to make a Light Fruit Cake.

Set out ingredients until they are of room temperature. (This insures a lighter cake.) Preheat oven to 325°. If you have an electric mixer use it now, since this cake involves a great deal of beating. At high speed, cream 1 cup butter with 1⅔ cups sugar until light and fluffy. Add 5 eggs, one at a time, beating well after each addition. Sift 2 cups flour with ¼ teaspoon nutmeg. Dredge ½ cup of finely-minced candied orange peel with a little of the flour. Turn mixer to low speed and gradually add remaining flour. By hand, fold in the dredged orange peel, 1 teaspoon caraway seeds, and 2 tablespoons whiskey. Butter an 8- or 9-inch fluted tube pan, dust with 2 tablespoons fine dry bread crumbs, and shake out excess crumbs. (I prefer to dust with crumbs rather than flour when sticky fruits are in the batter. It minimizes the chance that the cake will stick to the pan.) Bake for 1 hour, or until a cake tester comes out clean when inserted in the center of the cake. Turn out onto a cake rack to cool.

1 cup butter	1 teaspoon caraway seeds
1⅔ cups sugar	2 tablespoons whiskey
5 eggs	2 tablespoons fine dry bread
2 cups flour	crumbs
¼ teaspoon nutmeg	
½ cup finely-minced candied	
orange peel	YIELD: 12 servings

21

Andalusia (Kirsch Nut Ring)

Preheat oven to 375°. In the small bowl of the electric mixer, beat 4 egg whites until foamy. Gradually add ⅓ cup sugar, then 6 tablespoons potato starch (or cornstarch), continuing to beat until the mixture is thick and glossy. In the large bowl of the electric mixer, place 1¼ cups ground almonds, 2 tablespoons water, ½ cup less 1 tablespoon sugar, and 4 egg yolks, and beat for 2 minutes. (Beat the whites first, then beat the rest of the batter; you don't have to bother removing the beaters to clean them. If you beat the batter first, you must clean the beaters before you beat egg whites, or they won't get stiff.) Fold the egg-white mixture into the batter. Grease a 2-quart ring mold and dust with 2 tablespoons fine dry bread crumbs. Pour in the batter, and bake for 25 minutes. Turn out onto a rack to cool.

When the cake has cooled for ½ hour, split it in half, horizontally. Spread ¼ cup thick currant jam on bottom layer, and replace top. Cook ¼ cup sugar with 2 tablespoons water until sugar is dissolved. Remove from heat, add 6 tablespoons kirsch, and spoon this syrup over the cake. Place the cake on a platter and decorate the top with 6 candied cherries, halved. At servingtime, fill center with a double recipe *Crème Pâtissière* (see Index), to which you have added ¼ cup kirsch.

4 egg whites	¼ cup thick currant jam
⅓ cup sugar	¼ cup sugar
6 tablespoons potato starch, or cornstarch	2 tablespoons water
	6 tablespoons kirsch
1¼ cups ground almonds	6 candied cherries
2 tablespoons water	Double recipe *Crème Pâtissière*
½ cup less 1 tablespoon sugar	(see Index)
4 egg yolks	¼ cup kirsch
2 tablespoons fine dry bread crumbs	
	YIELD: 8 servings

Simnel Cake (Almond Paste Fruit Cake)

There are many versions of the origin of the name of this English cake, including a tale that involves one, Simon, and his wife, Nell. Not being in a position to vouch for the authenticity of anything so many generations ago, I endorse none. I *do* endorse the cake.

First, make an almond paste: In a bowl, mix 2½ cups of ground blanched almonds, ¾ cup sugar, 1 cup confectioners' sugar, 1 egg, 1 tablespoon rum, and 1 teaspoon almond extract, until the mixture is pasty.

Preheat oven to 325°. Cream ¾ cup butter with ¾ cup brown sugar until light and fluffy. Add 3 eggs, one at a time, beating well after each addition. Sift 2 cups flour with 1 teaspoon each cinnamon and nutmeg. Dissolve ½ teaspoon baking soda in ¼ cup milk, and add to the batter alternately with the sifted dry ingredients. Fold in 1½ cups currants, ¾ cup light raisins, ¼ cup diced candied lemon peel, and ⅓ cup slivered blanched almonds.

Divide the almond paste, above, in half. Roll each piece between 2 sheets of waxed paper, to a 9-inch circle. Pour ⅓ of the batter into a greased 9-inch spring-form pan. Peel the top piece of waxed paper from one of the circles of almond paste. With a thin sharp knife, loosen the paste from the bottom piece of paper. Place the rolling pin on the center of the paste, carefully fold the paste in half over the pin, lift it, and place over the batter in the pan. Pour in another ⅓ of the batter, repeat with the second circle of almond paste, and pour in remaining batter. Bake for 1¾ hours, or until a cake tester inserted in the center of the cake comes out clean. Cool the cake in the pan. Remove to a cake rack, and glaze the top with ½ cup confectioners' sugar moistened with just enough rum to bring it to a spreading consistency. When the glaze is dry, wrap the cake in foil, and store in the refrigerator for a day before slicing. Wrapped in foil, the cake will keep for weeks in the refrigerator.

2½ cups ground blanched almonds
¾ cup sugar
1 cup confectioners' sugar
1 egg
1 tablespoon rum
1 teaspoon almond extract
¾ cup butter
¾ cup brown sugar
3 eggs
2 cups flour

1 teaspoon cinnamon
1 teaspoon nutmeg
½ teaspoon baking soda
¼ cup milk
1½ cups currants
¾ cup light raisins
¼ cup diced candied lemon peel
⅓ cup slivered blanched almonds
½ cup confectioners' sugar
Rum

YIELD: 20 to 24 servings

Scotch Black Bun (Fruit Cake in a Crust)

A fruit cake baked in a crust is somewhat of a curiosity, and why it is called a bun, I couldn't say. Bake it at least two weeks ahead of time, to allow for ripening. One caution: No matter how carefully you slice the cake, it tends to crumble.

In a bowl, using a pastry blender or 2 knives, cut ⅔ cup butter into 1⅓ cups flour mixed with ⅓ teaspoon baking powder, until crumbs are formed. Gradually add 4 tablespoons of ice water, and blend to a smooth dough. Grease a long narrow bread pan, about 4½ by 12½ inches. On a lightly floured board, roll out ¾ of the dough to a rectangle large enough to line the pan. Roll out the remaining dough to a rectangle large enough to cover the top.

Preheat oven to 300°. Line the pan with the larger rectangle of dough. In a large bowl, put 1 pound of seeded raisins, 1 pound of currants, ¾ cup of chopped blanched almonds, and ½ cup sugar. Into the bowl, sift 1½ cups flour with ½ teaspoon cream of tartar, ½ teaspoon baking soda, 2 teaspoons ginger, 2 teaspoons allspice, and 2 teaspoons cinnamon. With your hands, mix all the ingredients. Add ½ cup milk, and mix together thoroughly. Pour into the pastry-lined pan, and press down with the back of a spoon. Cover with the top crust, seal edges well, and prick the top surface with a fork. With a small sharp knife, cut 6 evenly-spaced vents in the crust. Bake for 1½ hours. Cool in the pan. With the aid of a small funnel, pour 1 tablespoon brandy into each vent. Remove cake from pan, wrap in waxed paper or foil, and store in an airtight pan for two weeks before using.

⅔ cup butter	1½ cups flour
1⅓ cups flour	½ teaspoon cream of tartar
⅓ teaspoon baking powder	½ teaspoon baking soda
4 tablespoons ice water	2 teaspoons ginger
1 pound seeded raisins	2 teaspoons allspice
1 pound currants	2 teaspoons cinnamon
¾ cup chopped blanched almonds	½ cup milk
½ cup sugar	6 tablespoons brandy

YIELD: 20 servings

Cake of the *Bodega* (Orange Nut Cake)

Preheat oven to 350°. Cream 1 cup butter with 1 cup sugar until the mixture is light and fluffy. Add 3 egg yolks, and continue beating. Sift 2 cups flour with 1 teaspoon each baking powder and baking soda. Add to the batter alternately with 1 cup sour cream, beginning and ending with dry ingredients. Stir in the grated rind of 1 orange and ¼ cup each walnuts and pistachio nuts, coarsely chopped. Beat 3 egg whites until stiff but not dry, fold into the batter, and pour into a greased 9-inch tube pan. Bake for 55 minutes, or until a cake tester inserted in the center of the cake comes out clean. Mix ½ cup sugar with ¼ cup orange juice and ⅓ cup sweet sherry, and spoon over the hot cake in the pan. Let cake cool in pan before turning out onto a platter.

1 cup butter	Grated rind of 1 orange
1 cup sugar	¼ cup walnuts
3 egg yolks	¼ cup pistachio nuts
2 cups flour	3 egg whites
1 teaspoon baking powder	½ cup sugar
1 teaspoon baking soda	¼ cup orange juice
1 cup sour cream	⅓ cup sweet sherry

YIELD: 8 to 10 servings

Fröken Dohrman's Apple Cake

Preheat oven to 350°. Cream ¼ pound butter with 1 cup sugar until light and fluffy. Add 2 eggs, and beat well. Sift 1½ cups flour with 2 teaspoons baking powder, and add to the batter alternately with ½ cup milk. Beat until smooth, and pour into a greased 9-inch spring-form pan. Peel, core, and slice 3 medium-size cooking apples, and arrange them in concentric circles over the top of the batter. (To fit all the fruit on the cake, place the slices, rounded side up, and almost at right angles to the batter.) Mix 2 tablespoons sugar with ½ teaspoon cinnamon, and sprinkle over the fruit. Bake for 60 minutes, remove from the oven, and cool in the pan.

¼ pound butter	½ cup milk
1 cup sugar	3 medium-size cooking apples
2 eggs	2 tablespoons sugar
1½ cups flour	½ teaspoon cinnamon
2 teaspoons baking powder	

YIELD: 10 to 12 servings

Bischofsbrot
(Chocolate-Studded Fruit and Nut Loaf)

Literally translated, this is Bishop's Bread; in my house, it's
cake!

Preheat oven to 350°. Beat 5 egg yolks with 3 tablespoons of
sugar until thick and light. In a bowl, put ½ cup pitted dates,
cut into thirds, ½ cup slivered blanched almonds, ½ cup raisins, and ½ cup chocolate bits. Dredge with 2 tablespoons
flour, and fold into the yolk mixture. Sift ¼ cup flour with 2
tablespoons cocoa, and fold into the batter. Beat 5 egg whites
until they form moist peaks, gradually add ⅓ cup sugar, continuing to beat until thick and shiny. Fold into the batter, and
spoon into a greased and floured loaf pan, about 4½ by 12½
inches. Bake for 45 minutes, or until the cake starts to shrink
from the sides of the pan. Turn out onto a cake rack to cool.
Bischofsbrot keeps well in an airtight container.

5 egg yolks	½ cup chocolate bits
3 tablespoons sugar	2 tablespoons flour
½ cup pitted dates	¼ cup flour
½ cup slivered blanched	2 tablespoons cocoa
almonds	5 egg whites
½ cup raisins	⅓ cup sugar

YIELD: 12 servings

Cottage Cheese *Stollen*

I discovered the nucleus of this recipe in an old German cook-
book, and developed it to my satisfaction. Unlike most *stollen,*
it is made with baking powder, and the cheese was also a sur-

prising ingredient to me. Wrapped in foil or a plastic bag, it keeps indefinitely in the refrigerator, and my refrigerator is never without one.

Preheat oven to 325°. On a pastry board put: 1⅔ cups flour, 1½ teaspoons baking powder, ⅓ cup sugar, ½ teaspoon powdered cardamom, ¼ teaspoon nutmeg, ⅛ teaspoon salt, ½ cup plus 2 tablespoons cottage cheese, 6 tablespoons butter, 6 tablespoons ground almonds, ½ cup each seeded and seedless raisins, 2 ounces citron, slivered or diced. Make a well in the center of the dry ingredients, and drop in 1 egg and ¼ teaspoon each vanilla and almond extract. With your hands, mix everything together to a smooth dough. (This is a little messy, but by far the best system.) Pat out to a 6-by-10-inch rectangle. Fold over ⅓ of the dough from the long side (to make a 4-by-10-inch loaf). Place on a greased baking sheet, and bake for 45 minutes. Brush the top with 1 tablespoon soft butter, and dust with 3 tablespoons sifted powdered sugar. Cool on a cake rack, wrap in foil or a plastic bag, and refrigerate for two weeks before using.

1⅔ cups flour	6 tablespoons ground almonds
1½ teaspoons baking powder	½ cup seeded raisins
⅓ cup sugar	½ cup seedless raisins
½ teaspoon powdered carda-	2 ounces citron
mom	1 egg
¼ teaspoon nutmeg	¼ teaspoon vanilla
⅛ teaspoon salt	¼ teaspoon almond extract
½ cup plus 2 tablespoons cot-	1 tablespoon soft butter
tage cheese	3 tablespoons sifted confection-
6 tablespoons butter	ers' sugar

YIELD: 12 to 16 servings

Pain de Gênes (Almond Cake)

Here again, is a difference in concept (see *Bischofsbrot*). In French, *pain* is bread, but as far as I can see, this is a wonderful tea cake.

Preheat oven to 375°. Melt 5 tablespoons of butter, and cool. (Two minutes or so in the freezer will do it.) Beat 2 eggs and 2 egg yolks with ½ cup sugar and 2 tablespoons Vanilla Sugar (see Index) until thick and light. Mix ⅓ cup potato starch (or cornstarch) with 1¾ cups finely ground almonds, and fold into the egg-sugar mixture. (For this cake, the nuts must be reduced almost to a powder; a blender is really a *must* to get them fine enough.) Fold in 2 tablespoons Grand Marnier, and lastly the cooled butter. Grease an 8-inch layer-cake pan, line the bottom with waxed paper, and grease the paper. Pour in the batter, and bake for 25 to 30 minutes, until the cake just starts to shrink from the sides of the pan. (This cake must not be overbaked.) Turn out onto a cake rack, peel off the paper, and cool.

5 tablespoons butter	⅓ cup potato starch, or cornstarch
2 eggs	
2 egg yolks	1¾ cups finely ground almonds
½ cup sugar	2 tablespoons Grand Marnier
2 tablespoons Vanilla Sugar (see Index)	

YIELD: 8 servings

TORTEN

Dobosch Torte (Seven Layer Cake)

Sacher Torte (Viennese Chocolate Cake)

Linzer Torte (Jam-Filled Nut Tart)

Frau Baronin's Torte (Chocolate Nut Cake)

Cheese *Torte* from Berne

Hazelnut *Torte*

Carla's Chocolate Cake

Himbeerschaumtorte
(Meringue Layer Cake with Raspberries)

Carrot *Torte*

Skånetårta (Glazed Apple Almond Cake)

Baumkuchen (Tree Cake)

Tivolitårta (Nut-Meringue Layer Cake)

Dobosch Torte (Seven Layer Cake)

Dobosch Torte must be made a day ahead to achieve perfect texture and blending of flavors. There are many versions of this recipe, all essentially the same, but with minor variations. This is an excellent version, given to me by an elderly Hungarian lady who learned it from her grandmother.

First, make Chocolate Butter Cream (see Index) and refrigerate it for 1½ hours to achieve a spreading consistency.

Preheat oven to 400°. Separate 7 eggs. Beat the yolks with ¾ cup sugar until very thick and light. Beat the whites until stiff but not dry, and fold into the yolk mixture alternately with 1⅛ cups flour, sifted. Spread a generous ¼ cup of batter on the greased and floured bottom of a 9-inch spring-form pan or the back of a 9-inch layer-cake pan, making sure that the batter stays within ¼ inch of the edge. Bake for 6 minutes, or until pale gold. With a sharp knife, remove the layer from the pan immediately. Repeat until all the batter is used up; you should have 7 or 8 layers in all.

Caramelize ⅔ cup sugar by cooking it over low heat in a small heavy pan until sugar dissolves and turns golden. Quickly spread the caramel on one layer and set aside.

Assemble the *torte* when the butter cream is sufficiently firm. Spread it between layers, on the top layer, and around sides of the cake. Place the caramel-frosted layer on top and set the *torte* aside to ripen until the next day.

Chocolate Butter Cream (see Index)	¾ cup sugar
	1⅛ cups flour
7 eggs	⅔ cup sugar

YIELD: 12 to 16 servings

Sacher Torte (Viennese Chocolate Cake)

This is an Austrian classic attributed to a chef of the Hotel Sacher in Vienna. The number of recipes for this cake, all claiming to be the original, make you wonder if the chef ever told *anyone* his secret!

Preheat oven to 400°. With the electric beater, beat 6 egg whites until almost stiff. Gradually add ¾ cup sugar and continue to beat until meringue is thick and glossy. In another bowl, cream ½ cup butter. Add 1 cup chocolate bits, melted, and beat until fluffy. Gradually add ⅞ cup flour, sifted, beating very slowly until flour is incorporated, then at high speed for 1 minute. Turn to low speed, add meringue, and beat only until meringue is blended into chocolate mixture. Pour into a well-buttered and floured 8-inch spring-form pan, turn oven heat to 325°, and bake for 50 minutes, or until a cake tester comes out clean when inserted in center of cake. Cool cake in pan. Remove from pan, slice off crust-like top which develops during baking, and invert cake. Spread top and sides with ½ cup softened apricot jam, then frost over jam with Chocolate Frosting #2 (see Index).

6 egg whites	⅞ cup flour
¾ cup sugar	½ cup apricot jam
½ cup butter	Chocolate Frosting #2
1 cup chocolate bits	

YIELD: 8 servings

Linzer Torte (Jam-Filled Nut Tart)

An Austrian classic and worthy of preserving the tradition! Use the dough to make *Linzer* Cookies, too: Pinch off marble-sized balls of the dough, and roll them between the palms of your hands, making baguettes about 2 inches long with tapered ends. Bend these into crescent shapes, place them on lightly buttered cooky sheets, and bake them at 350° for 12 minutes or until golden.

For the *torte*, preheat oven to 325°. In a mixing bowl, combine 10 tablespoons butter, softened, ⅔ cup sugar, 1¼ cups flour, sifted, 1 cup ground almonds, 1 teaspoon grated lemon rind, ¼ teaspoon cinnamon, 2 egg yolks, and 2 hard-boiled egg yolks, mashed. With the fingers, work all ingredients to a smooth dough. Press half the dough into the bottom of a well-buttered 8-inch-square pan. Spread with 3 tablespoons softened apricot or raspberry jam. With palms of hands, on a lightly floured board, roll remaining dough into pencil-thick rolls. Press rolls lightly around sides of pan and in a lattice over jam-covered dough. Bake for 45 to 50 minutes, or until pale gold. Fill spaces between lattice with an additional 3 tablespoons of jam, and cut into 18 bars.

Linzer Torte may also be baked in a 9-inch pie plate or spring-form pan, and cut in wedges at the table.

10 tablespoons butter	¼ teaspoon cinnamon
⅔ cup sugar	2 egg yolks
1¼ cups flour	2 hard-boiled egg yolks
1 cup ground almonds	6 tablespoons apricot or rasp-
1 teaspoon grated lemon rind	berry jam

YIELD: 18 bars or 8 dessert servings

Frau Baronin's Torte (Chocolate Nut Cake)

Preheat oven to 350°. In the top of a double boiler, melt ½ cup chocolate bits. Separate 6 eggs, and beat the whites until stiff but not dry. In another bowl, without washing the beaters, beat 6 egg yolks and ¾ cup sugar until thick and light. To the beaten yolks, add 6 tablespoons fine dry bread crumbs, ¾ cup ground hazelnuts, and the melted chocolate. Beat for 2 minutes and fold in the stiffly beaten whites. Pour the batter into 2 greased and floured 9-inch layer-cake pans. Bake for 25 minutes. Turn the layers out onto cake racks, and cool.

Soften 2 tablespoons apricot jam with 1 teaspoon cognac, and spread on one layer. Beat 1½ cups cream until stiff with 2 tablespoons sugar. Spread a layer of the cream over the jam, place the second layer on top, and frost the top and sides of the cake with the remaining cream. Sprinkle 1 tablespoon grated bitter chocolate around the top.

½ cup chocolate bits	2 tablespoons apricot jam
6 eggs	1 teaspoon cognac
¾ cup sugar	1½ cups cream
6 tablespoons fine dry bread crumbs	2 tablespoons sugar
¾ cup ground hazelnuts	1 tablespoon grated bitter chocolate

YIELD: 8 to 10 servings

Cheese *Torte* from Berne

Preheat oven to 375°. Make ½ recipe Tart Dough (see Index), and press it on the bottom and ½ inch up the sides of an 8-inch spring-form pan. With a fork, prick the crust all over, and bake for 15 minutes. Remove from oven, and cool while making filling. Reduce oven heat to 325°.

In the large bowl of the electric mixer, place 18 ounces cottage cheese, 3 eggs, ⅔ cup sugar, 2 tablespoons cornstarch, ¾ cup heavy cream, and 1 teaspoon vanilla. Beat at high speed for 10 minutes. Scatter ¼ cup light raisins or ¼ cup finely chopped hazelnuts over crust, pour in filling, and bake for 45 to 50 minutes, or until almost set (the very center should not be quite set). Turn off heat, and leave cake in closed oven for 1 hour. Remove cake, cool completely in the pan, remove the sides of the spring-form pan, and place cake in refrigerator to chill.

½ recipe Tart Dough (see Index)
18 ounces cottage cheese
3 eggs
⅔ cup sugar

2 tablespoons cornstarch
¾ cup heavy cream
1 teaspoon vanilla
¼ cup light raisins or ¼ cup finely chopped hazelnuts

YIELD: 8 servings

Hazelnut *Torte*

Preheat oven to 325°. Beat 3 egg whites until they start to form moist peaks. Gradually add 3 tablespoons sugar, and continue beating until the meringue is very stiff. Beat 3 egg yolks with 3 tablespoons sugar until thick and light, and beat in 2 tablespoons brandy. Fold the meringue into the yolks, then fold in ½ cup hazelnuts, 3 tablespoons almonds, and 4 bitter almonds, all ground together. (If bitter almonds are unavailable, add ½ teaspoon almond extract to batter.) Pour into a greased 9-inch tube pan, and bake for 30 minutes, or until the top springs back when pressed lightly. Invert the pan on a rack until the cake is cool. Remove the cake, and frost with Cream Frosting (see Index), or Chocolate Frosting #1, #2, or #3 (see Index).

3 egg whites
3 tablespoons sugar
3 egg yolks
3 tablespoons sugar
2 tablespoons brandy
½ cup hazelnuts

3 tablespoons almonds
4 bitter almonds
Cream Frosting (see Index), or Chocolate Frosting #1, #2, or #3 (see Index)

YIELD: 6 to 8 servings

Carla's Chocolate Cake

Though the Viennese lady who gave me this recipe insisted that this was a cake, it must, by virtue of the almost complete absence of flour, be classified as a *torte*. Once you have sampled its flavor and texture, you will agree that it has earned a category unique to itself.

Preheat oven to 350°. In the top of a double boiler, melt 5 ounces of semisweet chocolate, turn into the bowl of the electric mixer, and cream with ¼ pound less 1 tablespoon of butter. Add 4 egg yolks, ½ cup sugar, and 1½ tablespoons sifted flour, continuing to beat until light and fluffy. Beat 4 egg whites until stiff but not dry, fold into batter, and pour into a well-greased and floured jelly-roll pan. Bake for 15 to 18 minutes, or until the center of the cake springs back when pressed lightly. Cool in the pan.

While the cake is baking, place another bowl in the freezer to chill. In the chilled bowl, whip 3 cups heavy cream until stiff with ⅓ cup sugar, and spread over cooled cake. (The cream must be very stiff; the chilled bowl helps.) Refrigerate cake at least 1 hour, so that the cream will be firm enough to hold icing.

While the cake is in the refrigerator, make the icing: In a saucepan, over medium heat, bring to a boil 1 tablespoon vegetable shortening, ½ cup black coffee, and ⅓ cup sugar. Add 4½ ounces semisweet chocolate, and 1 ounce bitter chocolate, and cook until chocolate is melted. Remove from heat, turn into the small bowl of the electric mixer, and beat at high speed for 8 minutes, or until thickened. Cool, but do not allow to set; if it begins to look set, stir with a spoon.

With a large spoon, apply icing over the whipped cream. This is rather tricky since the icing must be applied in a very thin layer, and demands time and patience. Spread it with the back of the spoon, and work on a small area at a time. When icing sets, cut cake into 15 squares. With a broad spatula, remove squares to a platter and refrigerate until servingtime. (If this seems more of a job than you wish to undertake, there is an alternative way of finishing the cake: Turn the baked cake out onto a board, and cut in half crosswise. Whip half the amount of cream and sugar, spread on half the cake, and cover with the other half. Make half the amount of chocolate icing, spread on top, and cut into 12 smaller squares.)

5 ounces semisweet chocolate	⅓ cup sugar
¼ pound less 1 tablespoon butter	1 tablespoon vegetable shortening
4 egg yolks	½ cup black coffee
½ cup sugar	⅓ cup sugar
1½ tablespoons sifted flour	4½ ounces semisweet chocolate
4 egg whites	1 ounce bitter chocolate
3 cups heavy cream	

YIELD: 12 to 15 servings

Himbeerschaumtorte
(Meringue Layer Cake with Raspberries)

If you prefer, make the meringue layers for this Viennese raspberry *torte* a day ahead, and store in a dry place; or, make them well ahead, and store in the freezer.

Preheat oven to 250°. Grease 2 cooky sheets or jelly-roll pans, line with waxed paper, and grease again. Using a 9-inch layer-cake pan as a guide, trace a circle on each sheet of paper. Beat 2 egg whites until foamy, gradually add ½ cup sugar, and continue beating until thick and glossy. Spread half the meringue on each circle to within ½ inch of the edge. (The meringue will spread during baking.) Bake for 20 minutes, turn off heat, and leave in closed oven for 1 hour, or until the paper peels easily from the meringue.

Whip 1 cup heavy cream until stiff with 3 tablespoons sugar. Clean and hull, but do not wash, 1 pint of raspberries. (This may seem very unhygienic, but the raspberries must be dry. I think of the many times I ate them straight from the vine; nothing happened!) Cut 12 ladyfingers in half lengthwise, and sprinkle with ¼ cup sherry or other sweet wine.

Place 1 of the meringue layers on a serving platter, and spread with ⅓ of the cream. Over the cream, arrange half of the ladyfingers like the spokes of a wheel, and fill in the spaces with half of the berries. Cover with another ⅓ of the cream. Make a second layer of ladyfingers and berries, alternating the position of the ladyfingers in relationship to the first layer. Cover with remaining cream, place the second meringue layer on top, and chill for 2 hours or more.

2 egg whites	1 pint raspberries
½ cup sugar	12 ladyfingers
1 cup heavy cream	¼ cup sherry or other sweet
3 tablespoons sugar	wine

YIELD: 10 to 12 servings

Carrot *Torte*

Preheat oven to 325°. In a meat grinder, using the finest blade, grind enough scraped carrots to measure 1 cup of pulp. Beat 6 egg yolks with 1 cup sugar until thick and light. Fold in the ground carrots, 1 cup of ground walnuts, ¼ cup fine dry bread crumbs, the grated rind of ½ lemon, and ⅔ cup light raisins.

Beat 6 egg whites until stiff but not dry, and fold into the batter. Pour into an ungreased 9-inch tube pan, and bake for 50 minutes, or until the top springs back when pressed lightly. Invert the pan on a cake rack until the cake is cool. Remove the cake from the pan, frost with 1 cup heavy cream whipped until stiff with 3 tablespoons sugar, and garnish with 12 perfect walnut halves.

Carrots	⅔ cup light raisins
6 egg yolks	6 egg whites
1 cup sugar	1 cup heavy cream
1 cup ground walnuts	3 tablespoons sugar
¼ cup fine dry bread crumbs	12 walnut halves
Grated rind of ½ lemon	

YIELD: 10 servings

Skånetårta (Glazed Apple Almond Cake)

Every time I see the Swedish lady who introduced me to Skånetårta, I marvel. She's so slim! For a party-size tårta (20 to 24 servings), triple the recipe, and bake in a 12-inch spring-form pan, baking dish, or heavy iron frying pan for about 65 minutes.

Peel, core, and slice 2 pounds of cooking apples. In a saucepan, dissolve ½ cup sugar in ½ cup water. Add the apples, cover, and cook until the fruit is just tender. Drain, and cool.

Line a greased 7-inch spring-form pan, baking dish, or heavy iron frying pan with foil, and grease the foil. Arrange the apple slices over the bottom. Preheat oven to 350°. Grind 1 cup of almonds with 6 bitter almonds. (Or, use 1⅓ cups of ground almonds, and add 1 teaspoon almond extract to the batter.) Cream 6 tablespoons butter with ½ cup sugar until light and fluffy. Add 3 eggs, one at a time, beating well after each addition. Fold in the ground nuts, reserving 1 tablespoon. Pour over the apples, and bake for 50 minutes. Cool in the pan until lukewarm, invert onto a platter, remove foil, and cool completely. Spread ¼ cup currant jelly over the apples, and sprinkle the reserved nuts around the edge. Whip 1 cup heavy cream until stiff with 2 tablespoons sugar, pour into a bowl, and pass separately.

2 pounds cooking apples	½ cup sugar
½ cup sugar	3 eggs
½ cup water	¼ cup currant jelly
1 cup almonds	1 cup heavy cream
6 bitter almonds	2 tablespoons sugar
6 tablespoons butter	

YIELD: 6 to 8 servings

Baumkuchen (Tree Cake)

Baumkuchen, or tree cake, derives its name from its similarity in appearance when the cake is cut to the cross-section of a tree trunk. In Europe, the cake was baked on a pole rotating in front of an open fire. As each layer was baked by the heat of the fire, another coat of batter was brushed on. With quite different equipment, I can achieve a similar result, though my layers are flat rather than cylindrical.

Preheat the broiler. (I use my portable rotisserie-broiler with excellent results.) Cream 1 cup plus 2 tablespoons each of butter and sugar. Add 9 egg yolks, the grated rind of 1 lemon, and 1 teaspoon vanilla, and beat thoroughly. Alternately fold in 1½ cups potato starch, sifted, and 9 egg whites beaten until stiff but not dry. Spread about ¼ cup of batter on the bottom of a greased 9-inch spring-form pan. Place about 6 inches from the heat and bake under the broiler until the surface looks dry, and is flecked with golden brown spots. Remove from the heat, spread with a second layer of batter, and bake as you did the first layer. (Once you start baking, the batter spreads very easily, because the cake and the pan are hot.) When half the batter is used up, lower the rack one shelf. (If the pan stays in the same place as you add layers, the surface is too close to the heat and will brown before it is well baked.) Continue baking until all the batter is used up; you should have about 12 to 14 layers.

Cool the cake before removing it from the pan. Mix 1½ cups confectioners' sugar with 3 tablespoons lemon juice, and spread over the top and sides of the cake. Serve in thin wedges.

1 cup plus 2 tablespoons butter	1½ cups potato starch
1 cup plus 2 tablespoons sugar	9 egg whites
9 egg yolks	1½ cups confectioners' sugar
Grated rind of 1 lemon	3 tablespoons lemon juice
1 teaspoon vanilla	

YIELD: 20 servings

Tivolitårta (Nut-Meringue Layer Cake)

There are all kinds of Danish pastries!

Preheat oven to 300°. Grease two 11-by-17-inch baking sheets, line with waxed paper, and grease again. Using an 8-inch layer-cake pan as a guide, trace two circles on each sheet of paper. Beat 6 egg whites until foamy, gradually add 1½ cups sugar, and continue beating until thick and glossy. Fold in 1 cup of ground almonds, walnuts, or hazelnuts. Reserve ⅓ of the mixture. Divide the remaining nut meringue among the 4 circles, and spread it evenly over each circle, almost to the edge. Bake for 45 minutes, or until the paper peels easily from the meringue. (The paper will not peel as readily from a nut meringue as a plain meringue. Grease the paper very generously.)

Cream ¼ pound sweet butter, add 1 teaspoon cocoa, and 1½ ounces bitter chocolate, melted, and mix well. Fold in a heaping spoonful of the reserved nut meringue, blend thoroughly, then fold in remaining meringue. Spread this mixture between the layers and on the top layer. Sprinkle 1 tablespoon of ground nuts (whichever you use in the meringue), over the top, and chill for 4 hours.

6 egg whites	1 teaspoon cocoa
1½ cups sugar	1½ ounces bitter chocolate
1 cup ground almonds, walnuts, or hazelnuts	1 tablespoon ground almonds, walnuts, or hazelnuts
¼ pound sweet butter	

YIELD: 8 to 10 servings

YEAST CAKES

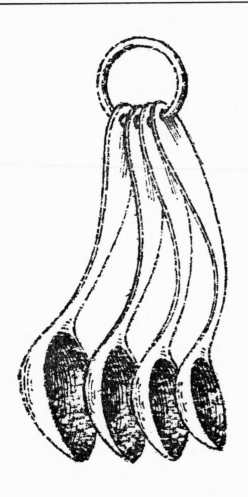

LARGE YEAST CAKES

———◆◆———

Pull-Aparts

Brioche aux Cerises (Cherry Custard Coffee Cake)

Kulich (Russian Easter Cake)

Syster Kaka (Custard-Topped Coffee Cake)

Borgmästare Fläta (Coffee Cake Braid)

Christollen

Gâteau Manon (Rich Layered Yeast Cake)

Kuglóf (Plain Coffee Cake)

Mistress Tinklepaugh's High Tea Loaf

Pull-Aparts

This traditional Hungarian coffee cake never bore the name Pull-Aparts, but that was what my husband's aunt called it, and you will see, when you serve it, why it is such a wonderfully descriptive name. That's precisely what you do; pull the cake apart with 2 forks. (Though, as my husband recalls Aunt Sally's weekly batch of Pull-Aparts, small boys rarely bothered with forks when fingers were so much handier.)

In a large mixing bowl, dissolve ½ package dry yeast in ¾ cup lukewarm milk. Add ¼ cup sugar, ¼ teaspoon salt, ½ teaspoon mace, 1 egg yolk, 4 tablespoons softened butter, and 1¾ cups flour. Beat until the dough leaves the spoon and the sides of the bowl clean. On a board, place ¼ cup flour, turn dough out on top of flour, and knead until flour is absorbed and dough is smooth. Place in a greased bowl, cover, and set in a warm place to rise for 2½ hours or until dough doubles in bulk.

Melt 4 tablespoons butter, and cool. Turn out risen dough onto a lightly floured board, and roll out to a rectangle ⅓ inch thick. With a 1½-inch round cutter, cut out as many circles of dough as possible. Gather the trimmings together, and reserve. In a small bowl, mix ⅓ cup walnuts, chopped, ¼ cup raisins, ¾ cup sugar, and 1 teaspoon cinnamon. Grease an 8-inch fluted tube pan, and dust with the sugar mixture. Place a layer of dough circles on the bottom of the pan, brush with cooled melted butter, and sprinkle generously with the sugar mixture. Repeat until all the dough and filling are used up, staggering the circles of dough so they are not directly on top of each other. Roll out the reserved dough trimmings to a thin sheet large enough to cover dough, place on top, and set in a

45

warm place to rise for 2 hours or until it doubles in bulk. When
it is almost risen, preheat oven to 375°. Bake for 35 minutes, or
until cake is golden brown. Turn out on a rack to cool.

½ package dry yeast	1¾ cups flour
¾ cup milk	¼ cup flour
¼ cup sugar	4 tablespoons butter
¼ teaspoon salt	⅓ cup walnuts, chopped
½ teaspoon mace	¼ cup raisins
1 egg yolk	¾ cup sugar
4 tablespoons softened butter	1 teaspoon cinnamon

YIELD: 8 servings

Brioche aux Cerises (Cherry Custard Coffee Cake)

Dissolve 2 teaspoons dry yeast in 2 tablespoons lukewarm water. Into a mixing bowl, sift together 2¼ cups flour, ¼ cup
sugar, and ⅛ teaspoon salt. Add 3 eggs, ½ pound less 2 tablespoons butter, softened, and the dissolved yeast. Beat with a
wooden spoon until the dough comes clean from the sides of
the bowl and the spoon. Cover, and set in a warm place for
about 3½ hours, or until dough has doubled in bulk.

While the dough rises, make a thick *Crème Pâtissière*. In a
saucepan, mix 3 egg yolks, ¼ cup flour, ⅓ cup sugar, and 1½
cups milk. Cook over low heat, stirring constantly, until cream
becomes very thick. Remove from heat, add 1 teaspoon vanilla,
and cool. Drain a 1-pound can of pitted light or dark cherries.

When the dough has risen, place it on a well-floured board.
Lightly roll ⅔ of dough to a circle ⅓ inch thick. Butter a
brioche mold, 7-inch spring-form pan, or deep cake pan and
line it with the dough, covering no more than ⅔ the height of
the sides. Spread the *Crème Pâtissière* over the bottom, cover
with cherries, and top with remaining dough rolled out to fit.

Press edges together, cover, and set in a warm place to rise for 2 hours. Shortly before baking time, preheat oven to 400°. Bake for 30 minutes. Unmold on a rack to cool. Dust with confectioners' sugar.

2 teaspoons dry yeast	3 egg yolks
2 tablespoons lukewarm water	¼ cup flour
2¼ cups flour	⅓ cup sugar
¼ cup sugar	1½ cups milk
⅛ teaspoon salt	1 teaspoon vanilla
3 eggs	1-pound can pitted light or dark
½ pound less 2 tablespoons	cherries
butter	Confectioners' sugar

YIELD: 10 to 12 servings

Kulich (Russian Easter Cake)

Dissolve 1 package dry yeast in ¼ cup lukewarm milk. In a large bowl, place ½ cup scalded milk, ¼ pound softened butter, ½ cup plus 1 tablespoon sugar, 1 egg, 1 egg yolk, ¼ teaspoon salt, 2 tablespoons vodka, and 2½ cups flour. With a wooden spoon, beat well. Add dissolved yeast, ¼ cup light raisins, ¼ cup dark raisins, ¼ cup chopped almonds, ¼ cup chopped candied orange peel, and beat again, until dough comes clean from the sides of the bowl and the spoon. Place ½ cup flour on a board, turn out dough on top of flour, and knead until the flour is absorbed and the dough smooth. Place in a greased bowl, and set in a warm place to rise for 2½ hours, or until dough doubles in bulk.

Punch down dough, shape into a ball, and place in a well-greased shortening can or large juice tin. (The traditional shape of *Kulich* is a tall cylinder). Set in a warm place to rise again for 1½ hours, or until dough doubles in bulk. When the dough is almost risen, preheat oven to 350°. Bake for 40 minutes. Cool on a rack, and frost top with ½ cup confectioners' sugar mixed with enough vodka to bring it to easy spreading consistency. Allow the frosting to dribble down the sides.

1 package dry yeast	2½ cups flour
¼ cup lukewarm milk	¼ cup light raisins
½ cup scalded milk	¼ cup dark raisins
¼ pound butter	¼ cup chopped almonds
½ cup plus 1 tablespoon sugar	¼ cup chopped candied orange
1 egg	peel
1 egg yolk	½ cup flour
¼ teaspoon salt	½ cup confectioners' sugar
2 tablespoons vodka	Vodka

YIELD: 12 servings

Syster Kaka (Custard-Topped Coffee Cake)

This is one of my favorite yeast doughs; light, tender, and moist. I never can make up my mind whether to make *Syster Kaka* with it, or use it for *Streusel* Apple Cake, (see Index). The solution is to divide the dough in half, and make both. The proportions below will make two cakes; one of each, or two of a kind. If one cake is all you want, make half of the following recipe.

Dissolve 2 teaspoons dry yeast in 1 tablespoon warm water. In a mixing bowl, place 4 tablespoons butter, cut in pieces, and 2½ tablespoons vegetable shortening. Scald ¾ cup milk, pour into bowl, and let cool until lukewarm. Add 1 lightly beaten egg, ¼ cup sugar, and ½ teaspoon each salt and powdered cardamom. Add dissolved yeast, and gradually beat in 2 cups flour, beating until dough is smooth and leaves the spoon and the sides of the bowl clean. Sprinkle 2 tablespoons of flour over the top, cover the bowl, and refrigerate overnight, or place in the freezer for 2 hours.

Turn dough out onto a lightly floured board, and knead well, adding a little flour if dough is sticky. Roll dough out into a 5-by-10-inch rectangle, spread with 1 tablespoon soft butter, and sprinkle with 1 tablespoon sugar, ¼ teaspoon cinnamon, and ¼ cup raisins. Starting from the long side, roll up jelly-roll fashion. Cut into 10 slices, and place, cut side up, in a greased 8-inch spring-form pan. Set in a warm place to rise for 1½ to 2 hours, until dough doubles in bulk.

While the dough is rising, make a custard: In a small saucepan, mix 1 lightly beaten egg, 1 tablespoon sugar, 1 teaspoon flour, and ½ cup milk. Cook over low heat, stirring constantly, until thick. Remove from heat, and cool until lukewarm.

When dough is almost risen, preheat oven to 350°. Spoon the custard over the risen dough, and bake for 40 minutes. Remove from pan, and cool on a cake rack.

2 teaspoons dry yeast	2 cups flour
1 tablespoon warm water	2 tablespoons flour
4 tablespoons butter	1 tablespoon butter
2½ tablespoons vegetable shortening	1 tablespoon sugar
¾ cup milk	¼ teaspoon cinnamon
1 egg	¼ cup raisins
¼ cup sugar	1 egg
½ teaspoon salt	1 tablespoon sugar
½ teaspoon powdered cardamom	1 teaspoon flour
	½ cup milk

YIELD: 6 to 8 servings

Borgmästare Fläta (Coffee Cake Braid)

Dissolve 1 package dry yeast in ½ cup lukewarm milk. (For all yeast dough, be sure the yeast is thoroughly dissolved before proceeding further.) Add ½ lightly beaten egg (reserve the rest), 2 tablespoons sugar, and 1⅓ cups flour, and mix thoroughly. Place ⅓ cup flour on a pastry board, turn dough out onto flour, and knead until flour is completely absorbed. Roll out to a narrow rectangle, ¼ inch thick and 15 inches long.

With your fingertips, mix ¼ pound plus 1 tablespoon butter with ½ cup flour. Pat this mixture over the half of the dough nearest to you. Fold the other half of the dough over toward you, and seal the 3 open edges. Roll out, away from you, until the dough is ¼ inch thick. Fold the third of the dough farthest away from you toward the center, then fold the third nearest you over the other layers, making 3 layers in all. Turn the dough one quarter of the way around, so that an open edge is nearest you. Roll, fold, and turn twice more. Roll out once more to the original, narrow, ¼-inch-thick rectangle, and cut into 3 long strips.

Mix ¼ cup sugar and ½ cup ground almonds, and sprinkle down the center of each strip. Press edges together to enclose filling. Braid the 3 strips together, and place on a greased baking sheet. Set in a warm place to rise for 1 hour. Shortly before the dough is risen, preheat oven to 375°. When the dough is risen, brush with reserved ½ egg, sprinkle with ¼ cup pearl sugar (available at fine food shops; if not available, use granulated sugar), and bake for 25 to 30 minutes until golden. Remove to a cake rack to cool.

1 package dry yeast
½ cup milk
½ lightly beaten egg
2 tablespoons sugar
1⅛ cups flour
⅓ cup flour
¼ pound plus 1 tablespoon butter

½ cup flour
¼ cup sugar
½ cup ground almonds
½ egg
¼ cup pearl sugar

YIELD: 8 servings

Christollen

Some years ago, a friend of mine sent me a *stollen* for Christmas. It was the finest I had ever tasted, and my request for the recipe was soon answered. Generally I copy recipes on index cards and discard the original; not so with this one. I cherish it. It is written in a "pinch of this, and just enough of that" style, except that here, "pounds" and "dozens" are involved. For instance, "5 pounds of flour" (and then she adds "or less"), and, "1 pound of raisins" ("or two"); and the dough should rise for 1 hour, or 2 or 3. Obviously, I had to do a good deal of work to make a usable recipe of it; and, since I wasn't cooking for a regiment, I reduced all the quantities. On only one point was she insistent: "Very important. *Stollen* should be four weeks old before you eat it (at least three weeks). I keep the *stollen* in a large, covered roaster. I have only one roaster, so I keep the other one wrapped up first in tin foil, then in old sheets and lots of paper, then a covered cardboard box. And the box and the roaster I store in a cold garage or unheated basement."

The preciseness of these directions, combined with the vagueness of the recipe, has always tickled me. My experience has shown that it does well, wrapped in foil or in a plastic bag, and stored in the refrigerator. The admonition to let it ripen for four weeks, or at least three, I well understand: Though it must ripen, it's much too good to be able to wait patiently that long.

Dissolve 1 package dry yeast in ⅓ cup warm milk. In a bowl, place 2⅔ cups flour, 7 tablespoons softened butter, ½ cup sugar, ¼ teaspoon salt, the grated rind of ½ lemon, ½ cup slivered almonds, ½ cup each dark and light raisins, ⅓ cup diced candied citron, and ⅓ cup warm milk. Add the dissolved yeast, and, with your hands, mix all ingredients. Turn out onto a lightly floured board, and knead for 10 minutes. Place in a greased bowl, cover, and let rise in a warm place for 2 to 3 hours until almost double in bulk. Turn out onto board, roll or pat out to a 7-by-9-inch rectangle. Fold over ⅓ of dough on top of the loaf (you now have a 4½-by-9-inch rectangle), with one side higher than the other. This is the traditional shape. Place on a greased baking sheet or in a greased 9-by-5-inch pan, and let rest for 10 minutes. Preheat oven to 350°. Bake for 40 minutes. Remove from oven, spread with 1 tablespoon butter, and sprinkle with ¼ cup confectioners' sugar. Cool on cake rack, wrap in foil or in a plastic bag, and store in refrigerator for three weeks before using.

Stollen keeps fresh for several months in the refrigerator.

1 package dry yeast	½ cup slivered almonds
⅛ cup warm milk	½ cup dark raisins
2⅔ cups flour	½ cup light raisins
7 tablespoons softened butter	⅓ cup diced candied citron
½ cup sugar	⅓ cup warm milk
¼ teaspoon salt	1 tablespoon butter
Grated rind of ½ lemon	¼ cup confectioners' sugar

YIELD: 12 servings

Gâteau Manon (Rich Layered Yeast Cake)

Dissolve 2 teaspoons of dry yeast in 6 tablespoons of warm milk. In a large bowl, beat 4 eggs. Add ¼ cup sugar, 10 tablespoons very soft butter, 2¼ cups flour, and the dissolved yeast, and beat very well with a wooden spoon. Cover the bowl, and set in a warm place to rise for 2 hours, or until double in bulk. Butter a 2- to 2½-quart deep baking tin (a fancy one, if you have it), and dust with fine dry bread crumbs. Pour in the batter, cover, and set in a warm place to rise for 1½ hours, or until double in bulk. When the batter is almost risen, preheat oven to 375°. Bake for 30 minutes. (If the top gets too brown toward the end of the baking, cover it with a piece of brown paper.) Remove the cake to a rack to cool.

While the cake is baking, make 1 recipe *Crème Pâtissière* (see Index), and ½ recipe Chocolate Butter Cream (see Index). Carefully, slice the cooled cake into 5 layers. Spread half the *Crème Pâtissière* on the bottom layer, cover with the next layer, and spread half the Chocolate Butter Cream on it. Repeat with the next 2 layers, and cover with the top layer. (If your cake is broader at the base than at the top, use more than half the filling for the 2 bottom layers.) Spread the top and sides of the reassembled cake with ½ cup softened apricot jam, and sprinkle with ⅓ cup slivered toasted almonds.

2 teaspoons dry yeast	1 recipe *Crème Pâtissière* (see
6 tablespoons warm milk	Index)
4 eggs	½ recipe Chocolate Butter
¼ cup sugar	Cream (see Index)
10 tablespoons very soft butter	½ cup apricot jam
2¼ cups flour	⅓ cup slivered toasted almonds
Fine dry bread crumbs	

YIELD: 12 servings

Kuglóf (Plain Coffee Cake)

Varying recipes for this type of not-too-sweet yeast cake are to be found all through the middle part of Europe. The name is always the same, though the spelling of *Kuglóf* changes from one country to another.

Dissolve 1 package of dry yeast in ½ cup lukewarm water.

Cream ¼ pound butter with ⅓ cup sugar. Add 4 egg yolks, one at a time, beating well after each addition. Add 2 cups flour, the grated rind of ½ lemon, 1 teaspoon vanilla, ¼ cup cream, ⅓ cup light raisins, and the dissolved yeast. With a wooden spoon, beat the dough vigorously until it is elastic and blisters. Generously grease a deep 9-inch tube pan (preferably fluted), and sprinkle with ⅓ cup slivered unblanched almonds. Spoon the batter into the pan, and set in a warm place to rise for 2½ hours, or until double in bulk. When the dough is almost risen, preheat oven to 350°. Bake for 40 to 45 minutes. Turn out onto a cake rack to cool, and dust generously with confectioners' sugar.

1 package dry yeast	1 teaspoon vanilla
½ cup lukewarm water	¼ cup cream
¼ pound butter	⅓ cup light raisins
⅓ cup sugar	⅓ cup slivered unblanched
4 egg yolks	almonds
2 cups flour	Confectioners' sugar
Grated rind of ½ lemon	

YIELD: 8 servings

Mistress Tinklepaugh's High Tea Loaf

Mix the yeast batter the night before: Sprinkle 1 package of dry yeast on ¼ cup warm water, and let it stand for 5 minutes. In the large bowl of the electric mixer, cream ½ pound butter with 2 tablespoons sugar. Beat in 3 egg yolks, the dissolved yeast, ½ teaspoon mace, and ¼ teaspoon salt. Add 2½ cups flour alternately with ¼ cup milk, and beat until the batter is smooth and elastic. Cover the bowl, and refrigerate overnight. (You may keep the dough in the refrigerator for several days.)

The next day, beat 1 egg white until foamy, gradually add

¾ cup sugar, continuing to beat until thick and shiny. Fold in ½ cup finely chopped walnuts, 1 cup raisins, and 2 teaspoons cinnamon. On a well-floured board, roll out the chilled dough to a 12-inch square, spread with the prepared filling, and roll up loosely, as for a jelly roll. Place in a well-greased large loaf pan (about 4½ by 11 inches), and set in a warm place to rise for 3 hours, or until almost doubled in bulk. When the dough is almost risen, preheat oven to 350°. Bake for 40 minutes, and turn out onto a cake rack to cool. Dust generously with confectioners' sugar.

1 package dry yeast
¼ cup warm water
½ pound butter
2 tablespoons sugar
3 egg yolks
½ teaspoon mace
¼ teaspoon salt
2½ cups flour

¼ cup milk
1 egg white
¾ cup sugar
½ cup finely chopped walnuts
1 cup raisins
2 teaspoons cinnamon
Confectioners' sugar

YIELD: 16 servings

SMALL YEAST CAKES

Berliner Krapfen (Jelly Doughnuts)

Cernosky (Nut Coffee Cakes)

Wiener Kipferl (Viennese Crescents)

Prune *Vdolky* (Doughnuts)

Streusel Apple Cake

Petits Babas aux Abricots (Cakes in Brandied Apricot Syrup)

Czechoslovakian Nut Slices

S.A.S. *Snurror* (Snails)

Edinburgh Cuts

Berliner Krapfen (Jelly Doughnuts)

Dissolve 1 package dry yeast in ⅓ cup lukewarm milk. Cut 5 tablespoons sweet butter into a mixing bowl. Pour ½ cup scalded milk over butter, and leave until butter is melted and mixture is lukewarm. Add 6 egg yolks, 4½ tablespoons sugar, ¼ teaspoon salt, 3 cups flour, and the dissolved yeast. With a wooden spoon, beat mixture until dough comes clean from sides of bowl and spoon.

On a floured board, roll the dough lightly to a thickness of ⅓ inch. With a 2-inch round cutter, cut out circles of dough, gather trimmings together, roll them out, and cut out more circles until dough is used up. Brush half the circles with milk. Place ½ teaspoon of any thick fruit jam on the center of remaining circles. Place a milk-brushed circle, brushed side down, on top of each jam-topped circle, and pinch edges together. Pat edges smooth. Place on lightly floured board, 2 inches apart, and set in a warm place to rise for 1 hour. Turn them over and let rise an additional hour. Fry in deep fat at 360°, cover pot for 3 minutes, uncover, turn *krapfen* and fry 2 minutes longer. Drain on absorbent paper, and dust generously with confectioners' sugar.

1 package dry yeast	¼ teaspoon salt
⅓ cup lukewarm milk	3 cups flour
5 tablespoons sweet butter	Thick fruit jam
½ cup scalded milk	Cold milk
6 egg yolks	Deep fat for frying
4½ tablespoons sugar	Confectioners' sugar

YIELD: about 20 doughnuts

Cernosky (Nut Coffee Cakes)

Dissolve 1 package of dry yeast in 2 tablespoons of lukewarm
water. Cut ¼ pound less 1 tablespoon butter into a mixing
bowl. Pour ¾ cup scalded milk over butter, and leave until
butter is melted and the mixture lukewarm. Add 1 egg yolk, ¼
cup sugar, ½ teaspoon each salt and almond extract, 2 cups
plus 2 tablespoons flour, ¾ cup currants, ½ cup chopped
toasted almonds and the dissolved yeast. With a wooden
spoon, beat mixture until dough comes clean from sides of
bowl and spoon. Cover bowl and set in freezer for 1½ hours.
(In pre-freezer days, chilled yeast dough was made the day before, and refrigerated overnight. Either way the results are
identical, so it's just a matter of which is more convenient for
you.)

Break off walnut-sized pieces of dough, roll into balls, and
place them 2 inches apart on well-buttered baking sheets. Set
in a warm place to rise until double in bulk, about 3½ hours.
When almost risen, preheat oven to 375°. Bake for 15 minutes.
While still hot, dip the cakes on all sides in ⅓ cup honey, then
roll in ½ cup ground almonds mixed with ¾ teaspoon cinnamon. Place on racks to dry. Serve warm; reheat if necessary.

1 package dry yeast	½ teaspoon almond extract
2 tablespoons lukewarm water	2 cups plus 2 tablespoons flour
¼ pound less 1 tablespoon butter	¾ cup currants
	½ cup chopped toasted almonds
¾ cup scalded milk	⅓ cup honey
1 egg yolk	½ cup ground almonds
¼ cup sugar	¾ teaspoon cinnamon
½ teaspoon salt	

YIELD: about 36 cakes

Wiener Kipferl (Viennese Crescents)

Early in the morning or the night before, dissolve 2 packages of dry yeast or 2 cakes of compressed yeast in ¼ cup of luke-warm milk. Into a mixing bowl, sift together 4½ cups flour, ¾ teaspoon salt, and ½ cup sugar. With a pastry blender, cut in ½ pound sweet butter. Add the grated rind of 1 lemon, 3 lightly beaten eggs, ½ cup sour cream, and the dissolved yeast. Knead until the dough comes clean from the sides of the bowl. Cover and refrigerate for 4 hours or overnight. (Or, make the dough early in the day, and set it in the freezer for 1½ hours.)

Divide dough into 8 parts. On a lightly floured board, roll out one part at a time to form a 9-inch round. Cut each round into 6 pie-shaped wedges. Put a spoonful of filling at the base of each wedge, roll up toward the point, bend into crescent shape, and place, 2 inches apart, on lightly buttered baking sheets. Brush the top of crescents with lightly beaten egg white, and set in warm place to rise until double in size (about 2 hours). Bake in preheated 350° oven for 15 minutes, or until golden brown.

To make filling, combine ½ cup currants, 1 cup sugar, 6 tablespoons butter, melted, 1 cup walnuts, chopped, ¼ cup heavy cream, 1 teaspoon vanilla.

2 packages dry yeast or 2 cakes compressed yeast	½ cup sour cream
¼ cup lukewarm milk	½ cup currants
4½ cups flour	1 cup sugar
¾ teaspoon salt	6 tablespoons butter
½ cup sugar	1 cup walnuts
½ pound sweet butter	¼ cup heavy cream
Grated rind of 1 lemon	1 teaspoon vanilla
3 eggs	1 egg white
	YIELD: 48 crescents

Prune *Vdolky* (Doughnuts)

Make the yeast dough for Jelly Doughnuts (see Index). On a floured board, lightly roll out the dough to a thickness of ½ inch. With a 2-inch round cutter, cut out circles of dough. Gather trimmings together, roll them out, and cut out more circles until dough is used up. Place the circles on the board, 2 inches apart, and set in a warm place to rise for 1 hour. Turn them over and let rise an additional hour.

While the dough is rising, cook 24 large, or 36 medium, prunes, in water to cover, until tender. Drain and pit the prunes, and purée through a sieve or food mill. To the purée, add 1 tablespoon lemon juice, and ¼ cup sugar. Sieve 1 cup cottage cheese into a bowl, add 1 teaspoon grated lemon rind, ¼ cup sugar, ¼ teaspoon vanilla, and mix well. Whip 1 cup cream until stiff with 3 tablespoons sugar.

When the circles of dough have risen on the second side, make a depression in the center of each, about ½ inch deep and ¾ inch in diameter. Fry in deep fat at 360°, cover pot for 3 minutes, uncover, turn *vdolky* and fry 2 minutes longer. Drain on absorbent paper. Just before serving, place a spoonful of cottage cheese in the depression in each *vdolky*, cover with the prune purée, and top with a spoonful of whipped cream.

Yeast dough for Jelly Doughnuts (see Index)
24 large, or 36 medium, prunes
1 tablespoon lemon juice
¼ cup sugar
1 cup cottage cheese

1 teaspoon grated lemon rind
¼ cup sugar
¼ teaspoon vanilla
1 cup cream
3 tablespoons sugar

YIELD: about 24 *vdolky*

Streusel Apple Cake

Make ½ recipe of the yeast dough used for *Syster Kaka* (see Index), and chill as directed. On a lightly floured board, roll out dough to a 9-by-12-inch rectangle, and place in a well-greased 9-by-12-inch pan. Set in a warm place to rise until dough doubles in bulk (1½ to 2 hours). Shortly before the dough is risen, preheat oven to 375°.

Peel and core 2 large baking apples (I like Rome Beauties), slice thinly, and arrange on top of the risen dough. In a bowl, with your fingertips, mix ¼ cup soft butter, ½ cup sugar, ½ cup flour, and ½ teaspoon cinnamon until the mixture forms crumbs. Sprinkle over apples, and bake cake for 20 minutes, then increase heat to 425°, and bake 5 minutes longer. Cool cake in pan, cut into 8 to 12 rectangles, and dust generously with confectioners' sugar.

½ recipe for yeast dough (see *Syster Kaka*)	½ cup sugar
	½ cup flour
2 large baking apples	½ teaspoon cinnamon
¼ cup butter	Confectioners' sugar

YIELD: 8 to 12 servings

Petits Babas aux Abricots (Cakes in Brandied Apricot Syrup)

Dissolve 2 teaspoons dry yeast in ¼ cup cold milk. Add 4 eggs, 2 tablespoons sugar, and 2¼ cups flour. Beat with a wooden spoon until the batter leaves the spoon and the sides of the bowl clean. Cover, and set in a warm place to rise for 1 hour.

While the dough rises, simmer 20 dried apricot halves, in

water to cover, for 15 minutes. Drain, cool, and cut into small pieces. With a wooden spoon, beat ¼ pound softened butter into the risen yeast dough until the butter is absorbed and the dough smooth. Carefully stir in the apricots without mashing them. Spoon the dough into 16 well-greased *baba* molds or custard cups, and set in a warm place to rise for about 2 hours, or until dough doubles in bulk. When dough has almost doubled, preheat the oven to 400°.

Bake the *babas* for 13 minutes, or until golden brown. While they are baking, cook 2 cups sugar and 2 cups water until the sugar is dissolved. Remove from heat, and add 1½ cups apricot brandy. Remove the cakes to a large platter. With a small sharp knife, make several 1-inch deep incisions in each cake. Spoon the brandy syrup over the cakes, and let them marinate in the syrup for several hours, basting occasionally. Beat 1 cup heavy cream until stiff, place in a small bowl, and pass separately.

Babas may also be served hot: Reheat in the syrup. Warm a jigger of brandy, ignite, and pour flaming over the *babas*. They are good, too, served hot or cold with ice cream, stewed fruit, or fresh berries.

2 teaspoons dry yeast	¼ pound butter
¼ cup cold milk	2 cups sugar
4 eggs	2 cups water
2 tablespoons sugar	1½ cups apricot brandy
2¼ cups flour	1 cup heavy cream
20 dried apricot halves	YIELD: 16 servings

Czechoslovakian Nut Slices

Unlike most yeast cakes, this dough does not rise before baking. Nevertheless, it produces a cake of good texture, with the characteristic yeast flavor. I like to serve it with a fruit compote.

Dissolve 1 package dry yeast in ¼ cup lukewarm milk. With a pastry blender or 2 knives, cut ½ pound butter into 4 cups flour. Add ½ cup sugar, ¼ teaspoon salt, 1 egg, 2 egg yolks, 1 cup sour cream, and the dissolved yeast. Mix together, then turn out onto a lightly floured board, and knead until the dough is smooth. Let the dough rest for 15 minutes while preparing filling. Preheat oven to 375°.

To make the filling, mix in a bowl: 1 pound of ground walnuts, 1 cup sugar, 1 teaspoon cinnamon, 1 tablespoon grated lemon rind, and 1 egg white.

On the pastry board, roll out the dough to a rectangle about 13 by 15 inches, and ⅓ inch thick. Cut into 4 narrow strips, 15 inches long. Place a portion of the filling down the center of each strip, enclose the filling with the dough, overlapping a bit, and place, seam-side down, on two greased baking sheets. Bake for 20 minutes. Cool on the sheets, dust with confectioners' sugar, and cut into 1-inch slices.

1 package dry yeast	1 cup sour cream
¼ cup lukewarm milk	1 pound ground walnuts
½ pound butter	1 cup sugar
4 cups flour	1 teaspoon cinnamon
½ cup sugar	1 tablespoon grated lemon rind
¼ teaspoon salt	1 egg white
1 egg	Confectioners' sugar
2 egg yolks	

YIELD: about 5 dozen slices

S.A.S. *Snurror* (Snails)

Several years ago, on a breakfast flight from Stockholm to Amsterdam, I was served the most delicious coffee cakes, and, having nothing better to do after breakfast, I availed myself of the airline stationery, and started off, "Dear S.A.S." The recipe for the snails or *schnecken* was waiting for me when I returned home. With typical Scandinavian thoroughness, they had enclosed an extra piece of paper, demonstrating the manner of folding the pastry to incorporate the shortening.

In a large bowl, dissolve 2 packages dry yeast in ⅔ cup cold milk and ¼ cup cold water. Melt 2 tablespoons cocoa butter (available at drugstores; if not, substitute butter) and cool. To the dissolved yeast add the cooled butter, 2 tablespoons sugar, 1 lightly beaten egg, ½ teaspoon salt, 1 teaspoon powdered cardamom, and 2½ cups flour. With a wooden spoon, mix to a smooth dough. Place ¾ cup flour on a pastry board, turn dough out onto flour, and knead until flour is absorbed. Roll dough out to a rectangle ¼ inch thick, and cover ⅔ of the surface with ¾ pound margarine, cut into small pieces. Fold the uncovered third of the dough over the center third, then fold these 2 layers over the last third, making 3 layers in all. Seal open edges by pressing with your fingers. Roll dough out to a rectangle ½ inch thick, and fold into 3 equal layers again. Flour the board if dough sticks. Repeat the rolling and folding twice more, and refrigerate for ½ hour.

Roll dough out to a long narrow rectangle ⅓ inch thick, sprinkle with ¾ cup sugar, 1 teaspoon cinnamon, and ¾ cup raisins. Starting from the long side, roll up, jelly-roll fashion. Cut into 24 equal-sized slices, and place, cut-side up and 2 inches apart, on greased baking sheets. With the palm of your hand, flatten each slice until it is a scant ½ inch thick. Re-

frigerate for 2 hours, or place in freezer for ½ hour. When the
chilling time is almost up, preheat oven to 400°. Bake for 13 to
17 minutes until golden.

Snurror are best fresh-baked. You may prepare them early in
the day, or the day before, and keep them in the refrigerator
on the baking sheets. If possible, bake them no more than an
hour or two before they are to be served.

2 packages dry yeast	2½ cups flour
⅔ cup cold milk	¾ cup flour
¼ cup cold water	¾ pound margarine
2 tablespoons cocoa butter	¾ cup sugar
2 tablespoons sugar	1 teaspoon cinnamon
1 egg	¾ cup raisins
½ teaspoon salt	
1 teaspoon powdered carda-	
mom	

YIELD: 24 snails

Edinburgh Cuts

Dissolve 1 package dry yeast in 2 tablespoons warm water. In
a large bowl, place ¼ pound butter, cut in pieces, ⅓ cup
sugar, ½ teaspoon salt, ¾ cup scalded milk, and ¼ cup light
cream. Stir with a wooden spoon until the butter is melted.
Add 2 eggs, 1 egg yolk (reserve the white), 1 teaspoon ginger, the grated rind of 1 orange, 3½ cups flour, and the dissolved yeast. Beat vigorously until the dough comes clean from
the sides of the bowl and the spoon. Put ½ cup flour on a pastry board, turn out the dough on top of the flour, and knead
until the flour is absorbed and the dough smooth. Place in a
greased bowl, and set in a warm place to rise for 1½ to 2
hours, or until double in bulk.

While the dough is rising, make the filling and the topping. To make the filling, mix together ¾ cup finely chopped walnuts, ⅔ cup fine bread crumbs, 1 cup brown sugar, 1 teaspoon ginger, and 1 egg beaten lightly with the reserved egg white.

To make the topping, cream ¼ pound butter with ½ cup brown sugar. Stir in 1½ cups light corn syrup and 1 cup coarsely chopped walnuts.

Grease two 10-by-15-inch jelly-roll pans. Divide the risen dough into 4 pieces. On a lightly floured board, roll out 2 pieces into rectangles large enough to fit the pans. Place 1 piece in each pan, and spread with the filling. Roll out the remaining 2 pieces the same way, and place over the filling. Spread the topping over the dough, and set the pans in a warm place to rise for 1 hour, or until double in bulk. When the dough is almost risen, preheat oven to 350°. Bake for 25 to 30 minutes, or until the cake just starts to shrink from the sides of the pans. Cool in the pans, and cut each cake into 24 squares.

1 package dry yeast	½ cup flour
2 tablespoons warm **water**	¾ cup finely chopped walnuts
¼ pound butter	⅔ cup fine bread crumbs
⅓ cup sugar	1 cup brown sugar
½ teaspoon salt	1 teaspoon ginger
¾ cup scalded milk	1 egg
¼ cup light cream	1 egg white
2 eggs	¼ pound butter
1 egg yolk	½ cup brown sugar
1 teaspoon ginger	1½ cups light corn syrup
Grated rind of 1 orange	1 cup coarsely chopped walnuts
3½ cups flour	

YIELD: 48 squares

SMALL CAKES
AND TARTLETS

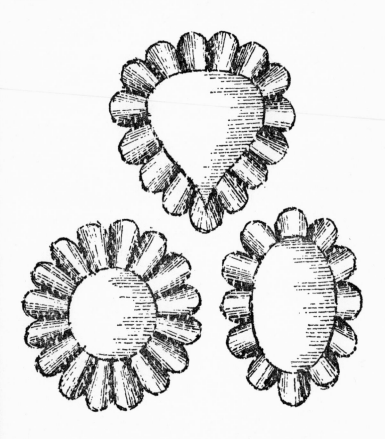

SMALL CAKES AND TARTLETS

Galette Béarnaise (Pearl Sugar Pastries)

Chocolatines

Mazariner (Almond Tarts see *Mazarintårta,* p. 113)

Tarteletas de la Marquesa Louria
(Mandarin Orange Coconut Tarts)

Utrecht Cakes (Frosted Chocolate Squares)

Hansi's *Schnitten* (Nut Meringue Slices)

Les Massillons (Glazed Almond Cakes)

Tartelettes aux Raisins (Grape Tarts)

Gevüld Speculaas (Dutch Christmas Cakes)

Indianer (Cream-Filled Cakes with Chocolate Frosting)

Galette Béarnaise (Pearl Sugar Pastries)

In a mixing bowl, place 2 cups flour, ½ pound butter, 1 egg yolk, 1½ tablespoons brandy, and 1 teaspoon orange flower water (available at a drugstore). With your fingers, work the ingredients to a smooth dough. Chill for ½ hour. On a lightly floured board, roll dough out to a thickness of ⅓ inch, fold in half, and chill for 15 minutes. Repeat rolling, folding, and chilling two more times.

Preheat oven to 350°. Butter a 9-inch layer-cake pan. Roll out a quarter of the dough to a 9-inch circle, place on the bottom of the pan, and sprinkle with 3 tablespoons of pearl sugar (granulated sugar will do, but the texture is not as good in this cake). Using remaining dough, add three more layers in the same way, but on the top layer sprinkle 2 tablespoons of very fine granulated sugar instead of pearl sugar. With the tines of a fork, press all around the edge of the pastry. Bake for 1 hour and 10 minutes, remove from pan, and cool on a cake rack. Serve this rich pastry in very small wedges.

2 cups flour	1 teaspoon orange flower water
½ pound butter	9 tablespoons pearl sugar
1 egg yolk	2 tablespoons very fine granu-
1½ tablespoons brandy	lated sugar

YIELD: 8 to 10 servings

Chocolatines

Preheat oven to 350°. Cream ¼ cup butter with ½ cup sugar until light and fluffy. Beat in 2 eggs and 1 tablespoon kirsch, then fold in ⅓ cup flour and 1 cup ground almonds. Spread batter in a well-greased 9-inch-square pan, and bake for 25 to 30 minutes, or until a cake tester, inserted in the center of the cake, comes out clean. Cool cake in the pan.

While the cake is baking, make ½ recipe Chocolate Butter Cream (see Index), and refrigerate. Cut cooled cake into 16 squares, and slice each square in half to make 2 layers. Spread the chocolate butter cream frosting on one layer, and sandwich the two layers together. Apply frosting around the sides, and dip each side into ½ cup slivered toasted almonds. Spread frosting on top, and sprinkle with a few more almonds. (At best this is a messy procedure, and takes patience, but one taste and all is repaid.) Refrigerate *Chocolatines* until butter cream is set.

¼ cup butter	1 cup ground almonds
½ cup sugar	½ recipe Chocolate Butter
2 eggs	Cream (see Index)
1 tablespoon kirsch	½ cup slivered toasted almonds
⅛ cup flour	

YIELD: 16 squares

Tarteletas de la Marquesa Louria
(Mandarin Orange Coconut Tarts)

Press 1 recipe Tart Dough (see Index) on the bottom and sides of 12 well-greased 3-inch muffin tins or fluted tart tins.

Preheat oven to 325°. Drain two 11-ounce cans of Mandarin oranges, and put the segments of fruit on the bottom of the prepared tins. Whip 3 egg whites until foamy, gradually add ¾ cup sugar and 1 teaspoon vanilla, continuing to beat until thick and shiny. Fold in 1½ cups flaked coconut, and spoon the meringue over the fruit. With the back of a teaspoon, seal meringue to the pastry so that it will not shrink from the crust during baking. Bake on the bottom shelf of the oven (to be sure that the bottom crust is well baked) for 30 minutes. Carefully remove from tins, and cool, upside down, on cake racks. (This crust is very tender. If you try to cool the tarts right side up, the weight of the fruit will cause the warm crust to collapse. The baked coconut meringue is solid enough to bear the weight.)

1 recipe Tart Dough (see Index)	3 egg whites
	¾ cup sugar
2 11-ounce cans Mandarin oranges	1 teaspoon vanilla
	1½ cups flaked coconut

YIELD: 12 servings

Utrecht Cakes (Frosted Chocolate Squares)

Preheat oven to 325°. In the top of a double boiler, melt 1 ounce bitter chocolate. Stir in ½ cup milk, remove from heat and cool to lukewarm. Cream ⅓ cup butter with ⅓ cup brown sugar. Add 1 egg, the melted chocolate, ¾ cup plus 1 tablespoon flour sifted with ½ teaspoon baking powder, and ½ teaspoon vanilla. Beat until smooth, and pour into a greased and floured 8-inch-square pan. Bake for 15 minutes. Cool in the pan, and spread with ½ recipe Chocolate Frosting #1 (see Index). When frosting is set, cut into 25 squares.

1 ounce bitter chocolate	¾ cup plus 1 tablespoon flour
½ cup milk	½ teaspoon baking powder
⅓ cup butter	½ teaspoon vanilla
⅓ cup brown sugar	½ recipe Chocolate Frosting #1
1 egg	(see Index)

YIELD: 25 squares

Hansi's *Schnitten* (Nut Meringue Slices)

The Viennese prove the theory that love and butter are the requisites of good cooking.

Preheat oven to 350°. In a bowl, using your hands, mix 2½ cups flour, ½ cup sugar, ½ pound sweet butter, and 2 egg yolks. When the dough is smooth, pat it evenly over the bottom of a 10-by-15-inch jelly-roll pan. Prick the dough with a fork, and bake for 15 to 20 minutes, or until pale gold.

Remove from the oven, and spread 1 cup raspberry jam over the surface. Beat 4 egg whites until foamy, gradually add 1 cup sugar, continuing to beat until very thick and shiny. Fold in 1½ cups of ground almonds or walnuts, and spread this nut meringue over the jam. Bake for 25 minutes, or until the top is golden. Cool in the pan, and cut into sixty 1-by-2½-inch bars. Store in an airtight tin.

2½ cups flour	4 egg whites
½ cup sugar	1 cup sugar
½ pound sweet butter	1½ cups ground almonds or
2 egg yolks	walnuts
1 cup raspberry jam	

YIELD: 60 bars

Les Massillons (Glazed Almond Cakes)

Preheat oven to 375°. In the small bowl of the electric mixer, beat together: 3 egg whites, ½ cup plus 1 tablespoon each ground almonds and Vanilla Sugar (see Index), ¼ pound plus 1 tablespoon butter, and 1 tablespoon potato starch. Don't worry if the mixture looks curdled. Grease twelve 2½-inch fluted tart tins or muffin tins, and dust with fine bread crumbs. Spoon a portion of the batter into each tin, and bake for 25 minutes. Remove from tins immediately, and cool. (Sometimes it is difficult to remove tarts or cakes from fluted tins. You may have missed a spot when you greased the tin. A wire cake tester or fine knitting needle is very useful to loosen them.) Spread ⅓ teaspoon apricot jam over the top of each little cake, then spread a glaze of ¼ cup confectioners' sugar mixed with 1 teaspoon kirsch, over the jam.

3 egg whites
½ cup plus 1 tablespoon ground almonds
½ cup plus 1 tablespoon Vanilla Sugar (see Index)
¼ pound plus 1 tablespoon butter

1 tablespoon potato starch
Fine bread crumbs
4 teaspoons apricot jam
¼ cup confectioners' sugar
1 teaspoon kirsch
YIELD: 12 small cakes

Tartelettes aux Raisins (Grape Tarts)

Don't be confused by the name; in French, grapes are called *raisins*.

With a supply of baked tart shells in your freezer, you can assemble a dessert in no time flat. Substitute any stewed or canned fruit, or uncooked, fresh berries, or fill the shells with *Crème Pâtissière* (see Index), and cover with fruit or berries.

Preheat oven to 350°. Make 1 recipe Tart Dough (see Index), divide the dough into 16 parts, and line sixteen 2½-inch tart tins or muffin tins, pressing with the balls of your thumbs to keep shells of even thickness. Prick the dough well with a fork, and bake for 15 minutes, or until golden. Remove the shells from the tins as soon as possible, since they get crisp quickly, and will break easily.

Stem 3 pounds of seedless grapes. In a saucepan, bring to a boil 1½ cups each sugar and water. Add the grapes, and bring to a boil again. Drain, and cool the fruit. Shortly before serving-time, mix the grapes with ¾ cup sieved apricot jam, spoon into the baked shells, and sprinkle with ¼ cup finely chopped pistachio nuts. (I prefer to fill them at the last minute so that the pastry stays crisp. This is particularly important in humid weather.)

1 recipe Tart Dough (see Index)
3 pounds seedless grapes
1½ cups sugar

1½ cups water
¾ cup sieved apricot jam
¼ cup finely chopped pistachio nuts

YIELD: 16 tarts

Gevüld Speculaas (Dutch Christmas Cakes)

These traditional Dutch Christmas cakes keep indefinitely in a tin in the refrigerator.

In a bowl, mix together: 2⅓ cups flour, 1¼ cups (packed) dark brown sugar, 2 teaspoons cinnamon, 1 teaspoon nutmeg, ½ teaspoon powdered cloves, ⅛ teaspoon powdered cardamom, and ½ teaspoon baking powder. With a pastry blender or 2 knives, cut in ⅔ cup butter, add 2 tablespoon milk, and, with your hands, blend to a smooth dough.

Make ½ recipe of almond paste (see *Simnel* Cake). There will be ½ egg left over; reserve it. Preheat oven to 350°. Press ⅓ of the dough on the bottom of a greased 8-inch-square pan. Spread the almond paste evenly over the dough, and cover with the remaining ⅔ of the dough. With a small pointed knife score the surface of the dough into 36 squares. (Score as you would a ham, penetrating the surface about ⅛ inch deep.) Brush the top of the dough with the reserved egg, place half a blanched almond on the center of each square, and brush the almonds with the egg. Bake for 50 minutes. Turn out onto a cake rack to cool. Cut into 36 squares.

2⅓ cups flour
1¼ cups (packed) dark brown
   sugar
2 teaspoons cinnamon
1 teaspoon nutmeg
½ teaspoon powdered cloves
⅛ teaspoon powdered cardamom

½ teaspoon baking powder
⅔ cup butter
2 tablespoons milk
½ recipe almond paste (see
   Simnel Cake)
½ egg
18 blanched almonds, halved

YIELD: 36 squares

Indianer
(Cream-Filled Cakes with Chocolate Frosting)

Despite the name, these are Viennese. *Indianer* are tradi-tionally baked in a type of muffin tin unlike ours; each depres-sion is a shallow half-sphere. When they are filled and paired together, the sphere shape is very pretty. You may, however, use any muffin tin you have.

Preheat oven to 350°. Beat 4 egg yolks with ½ cup sugar until very thick and light. Beat 4 egg whites until stiff but not dry, and fold into the egg-yolk mixture alternately with ½ cup flour, sifted. Spoon the batter into 20 well-greased and floured tins, above, and bake for 15 to 16 minutes, or until the top springs back when pressed gently. Remove from the tins, and cool on cake racks.

Carefully, scoop out a little of the cake from each muffin,

leaving a shell a generous ½ inch thick. Whip 1 cup heavy cream until thick with 3 tablespoons sugar. Spoon the cream into half the cake shells. Prepare Chocolate Frosting #1, #2, or #3 (see Index). Dip the outsides of the remaining shells into the frosting, and replace on the cake racks until the frosting is set. Place a frosted shell on top of each cream-filled shell, and press down gently. A border of cream should remain visible between the halves. Chill until servingtime.

4 egg yolks	1 cup heavy cream
½ cup sugar	3 tablespoons sugar
4 egg whites	Chocolate Frosting #1, #2, or
½ cup flour	#3 (see Index)

YIELD: 10 servings

COOKIES

COOKIES

Pignoli Cookies (Pine Nut Cookies)

Mandulás Kétszersült (Almond Zwieback)

Nötkulor (Cherry Nut Cookies)

Linzer Cookies (See *Linzer* Torte, p. 32)

Meringues (See Beignets à la Dijonnaise, p. 143)

Macaroons Cintra

Ebba's *Tattarbröd* (Gypsy Cookies)

Brunsli (Swiss Almond Bars)

Vera's Oatmeal Wafers

Miroirs (Nut Meringues)

Finnish Bridal Cookies

Bucuresti Hazelnut Cookies

Bratislavian Wafers

Kokosdrømme (Coconut Dreams)

Tosca Cookies

Dentelles (Lace Cookies, see *Les Dentelles de Luciê*, p. 207)

Pignoli Cookies (Pine Nut Cookies)

Preheat oven to 375°. Cream ½ cup butter with 2 tablespoons sugar and 2 tablespoons honey until light and fluffy. Beat in 1 cup flour and 2 teaspoons brandy. Add ½ cup pine nuts and mix with your hands to obtain a smooth dough. Break off marble-sized pieces of dough, roll into balls, and place 1 inch apart on a lightly buttered cooky sheet. Bake for 10 minutes, or until pale gold.

½ cup butter	1 cup flour
2 tablespoons sugar	2 teaspoons brandy
2 tablespoons honey	½ cup pine nuts

YIELD: about 28 cookies

Mandulás Kétszersült (Almond Zwieback)

Preheat oven to 400°. Spread ½ cup of slivered almonds on a cooky sheet and toast in the oven about 6 minutes, or until browned. Cream ¼ cup butter with ½ cup sugar. Beat in 2 eggs and 1 teaspoon almond extract, then fold in 1½ cups flour sifted with 1½ teaspoons baking powder. Add the toasted almonds, stir to distribute nuts evenly, turn out on a lightly floured board, and shape into a 13-inch long roll. Bake on a buttered cooky sheet for 18 to 20 minutes, or until golden. Remove from oven. Lower heat to 200°, leaving oven door open. Cut roll into slices ½ inch thick, cut each slice in half lengthwise, replace on cooky sheet, and dry in the oven, with the door closed, for 20 minutes. Turn off heat, leave zwieback in the oven 20 to 30 minutes longer, or until golden.

½ cup slivered almonds   1 teaspoon almond extract
¼ cup butter   1½ cups flour
½ cup sugar   1½ teaspoons baking powder
2 eggs

YIELD: about 50

Nötkulor (Cherry Nut Cookies)

Cream ¼ pound less 1 tablespoon of butter with ½ cup less 1
tablespoon of sugar. Stir in 1 egg yolk, ½ teaspoon almond extract, and ½ tablespoon each grated orange rind, grated lemon
rind, and lemon juice. Using fingers, blend in 1¼ cups of
flour. Work mixture to a smooth dough. Roll into 36 marble-
sized balls, dip into 1 egg white, slightly beaten, and roll in
⅓ cup of chopped blanched almonds. Preheat oven to 350°.
    Place balls 1½ inches apart on well-buttered cooky sheets.
Press half a maraschino cherry, cut side down, on top of each
ball and bake for 10 to 12 minutes, or until very pale gold.

¼ pound less 1 tablespoon   ½ tablespoon lemon juice
  butter   1¼ cups flour
½ cup less 1 tablespoon sugar   1 egg white
1 egg yolk   ⅓ cup chopped blanched
½ teaspoon almond extract   almonds
½ tablespoon grated orange   18 maraschino cherries
  rind
½ tablespoon grated lemon   YIELD: 36 cookies
  rind

Macaroons Cintra

Preheat oven to 325°. In a bowl, mix 1 lightly beaten egg, ½
cup less 1 tablespoon sugar, 3 tablespoons melted butter, and
1¼ cups flaked coconut, firmly packed. Drop by teaspoonful

onto a greased baking sheet, and bake for 10 minutes. Reduce heat to 250°, and bake 10 minutes longer.

1 lightly beaten egg	1¼ cups flaked coconut, firmly packed
½ cup less 1 tablespoon sugar	
3 tablespoons melted butter	YIELD: 20 macaroons

Ebba's *Tattarbröd* (Gypsy Cookies)

A Swedish friend gave me this recipe. In addition to producing a very good cooky, it gives me an opportunity to use up stale cooky crumbs. You may use zwieback crumbs instead; in fact, the original recipe specifies them.

In a mixing bowl, place 2½ cups flour, ¾ cup plus 2 tablespoons sugar, ½ pound less 2 tablespoons soft butter, 1⅓ cups cooky or zwieback crumbs, 1 lightly beaten egg, 1 teaspoon cinnamon, 1 teaspoon vanilla, and 1½ teaspoons pulverized ammonium carbonate. (This is a leavening agent that produces a wonderfully crisp texture; it is available at drugstores.) With your hands, mix to a smooth dough.

Preheat oven to 350°. Break off walnut-sized pieces of dough. On a board, roll with the palms of your hands until the dough is finger-thick. (It should be about ½ inch in diameter.) Cut into pieces 1½ inches long, roll in either granulated sugar or pearl sugar (available at food specialty shops), and place, ¾ inch apart, on well-greased cooky sheets. Bake for 10 to 12 minutes, or until the top just starts to feel firm.

2½ cups flour	1 egg
¾ cup plus 2 tablespoons sugar	1 teaspoon cinnamon
½ pound less 2 tablespoons butter	1 teaspoon vanilla
1⅓ cups cooky or zwieback crumbs	1½ teaspoons pulverized ammonium carbonate
	Granulated sugar or pearl sugar
YIELD: about 100 cookies	

Brunsli (Swiss Almond Bars)

"Li" at the end of a name is generally a giveaway that the name is of Swiss origin. *Brunsli* is no exception. Store these cookies in a covered box in the refrigerator to maintain the moist, chewy texture.

Beat 2 egg whites until foamy. Gradually add 1 cup sugar, 1 teaspoon cinnamon, and ¼ teaspoon powdered cloves, continuing to beat until thick. Fold in 1 tablespoon kirsch, 1½ ounces bitter chocolate, grated, and ½ pound ground almonds. Sprinkle 3 tablespoons sugar on a pastry board, turn the nut mixture out onto the sugar, and sprinkle 2 additional tablespoons sugar on top. With your hand, pat to an 8-by-12-inch rectangle, ⅓ inch thick. Dip a sharp knife into cold water, and cut into 48 1-by-2-inch rectangles. Dip the knife into water whenever the nut mixture begins to stick. With a spatula, lift the rectangles onto a greased baking sheet, placing them 1 inch apart. Set aside for 1 hour until the surface seems dry and a bit crusty. When the hour is almost up, preheat oven to 350°. Bake for 6 minutes. There should be a thin top and bottom crust, but the middle must be soft.

2 egg whites	1½ ounces bitter chocolate
1 cup sugar	½ pound ground almonds
1 teaspoon cinnamon	3 tablespoons sugar
¼ teaspoon powdered cloves	2 tablespoons sugar
1 tablespoon kirsch	

YIELD: 48 bars

Vera's Oatmeal Wafers

Preheat oven to 350°. In a bowl, place ¾ cup plus 1 tablespoon each flour, sugar, and old-fashioned rolled oats. Add ½ teaspoon baking powder, 1 teaspoon vanilla, ¼ pound plus 1 tablespoon butter, melted, 3½ tablespoons each light molasses and heavy cream. With a wooden spoon, mix thoroughly. Drop by half teaspoonfuls, 2½ inches apart, onto well-greased cooky sheets. (These cookies spread fantastically; bake about 12 on a sheet.) Bake for 8 minutes, and leave on sheets about half a minute longer, until cookies stiffen.

¾ cup plus 1 tablespoon flour	1 teaspoon vanilla
¾ cup plus 1 tablespoon sugar	¼ pound plus 2 tablespoons
¾ cup plus 1 tablespoon old-	butter, melted
fashioned rolled oats	3½ tablespoons light molasses
½ teaspoon baking powder	3½ tablespoons heavy cream

YIELD: about 8 dozen cookies

Miroirs (Nut Meringues)

Preheat oven to 350°. Separate 4 eggs, reserving 2 of the egg yolks. Beat the 4 egg whites until they stand in soft peaks. Gradually add ½ cup sugar and ½ teaspoon vanilla, continuing to beat until thick and shiny. Fold in 4 ounces of ground almonds. Spoon the meringue mixture into a pastry tube with a plain round opening, and pipe 1¼-inch mounds, 1 inch apart, on greased cooky sheets.

In a separate bowl, mix the 2 egg yolks, ¼ cup sugar, 2

tablespoons flour, 2 tablespoons soft butter, and 1 teaspoon rum. Add 4 ounces of almonds, finely chopped, and, with a teaspoon, put a small portion of the mixture on the center of each mound of meringue. Bake for 12 to 15 minutes, or until light brown around the edges. Remove to a cake rack to cool.

4 egg whites	¼ cup sugar
½ cup sugar	2 tablespoons flour
½ teaspoon vanilla	2 tablespoons butter
4 ounces ground almonds	1 teaspoon rum
2 egg yolks	4 ounces almonds

YIELD: about 3½ dozen cookies

Finnish Bridal Cookies

I suppose it's quite proper that bridal cookies should be paired, as the recipe states. Actually, they do look better that way, but I often leave them as single wafers, too. They are rich and delicately flavored; very good to have on hand in the freezer or the cooky jar.

Preheat oven to 375°. Beat 1 egg white until stiff. In a separate bowl, cream ¼ pound butter with ½ cup Vanilla Sugar (see Index) until very light and fluffy. Add ¾ cup flour, beat until smooth, then fold in the stiffly beaten egg white. Drop by rounded half teaspoonfuls, 1½ inches apart, on ungreased cooky sheets, and bake for 8 to 10 minutes until light brown around the edges. Remove cookies, and cool. Spread half of them with any thick jam or marmalade, or spread with ¼ recipe Chocolate Frosting #3 (see Index), and cover with remaining cookies.

1 egg white
¼ pound butter
½ cup Vanilla Sugar (see
    Index)

¾ cup flour
⅓ cup thick jam or marmalade,
    or ¼ recipe Chocolate Frost-
    ing #3 (see Index)

YIELD: about 24 paired, or 48 single, cookies

Bucuresti Hazelnut Cookies

In a bowl, put ¼ pound less 1 tablespoon butter, ¼ cup sugar,
½ teaspoon cinnamon, ½ teaspoon baking soda, 2 ounces
ground hazelnuts, and ¾ cup flour. With your hands, mix until you have a smooth dough, shape into a roll 1¼ inches in
diameter, and chill for 1 hour.

In a separate bowl, place 4 tablespoons butter, ½ cup flour,
and 1 tablespoon sugar. With your hands, mix these ingredients
to a smooth dough, and put into a pastry tube fitted with a
star-shaped opening.

When the first dough is chilled, preheat oven to 350°. Cut
the roll into slices ¼ inch thick, and place, 1 inch apart, on
greased cooky sheets. Press out the second dough in long strips,
cut into 1¼-inch pieces, and place a piece on top of each
cooky. Bake for 13 to 14 minutes.

¼ pound less 1 tablespoon
    butter
¼ cup sugar
½ teaspoon cinnamon
½ teaspoon baking soda

2 ounces ground hazelnuts
¾ cup flour
4 tablespoons butter
½ cup flour
1 tablespoon sugar

YIELD: about 4 dozen cookies

Bratislavian Wafers

These cookies can be made two ways. Generally, I divide the dough in half, and bake both variations.

Cream ½ cup butter with 1 cup Vanilla Sugar (see Index) until light and fluffy. Add 1 egg and 1 tablespoon cream, and beat well. Add 2 cups of flour sifted with 1 teaspoon baking powder, and mix well. Divide the dough in half, and add 2 tablespoons poppy seeds to one half. Place both portions of dough in the freezer for 1 hour.

Preheat oven to 350°. On a lightly floured board, roll out half of the plain dough a scant ⅟₁₆ inch thick. (The thinner you roll these cookies, the better they are.) With a long-bladed spatula, carefully loosen the dough from the board. (Otherwise, you will have difficulty moving them after they are cut.) With a pastry wheel, cut into 1-by-2-inch rectangles, and place, ½ inch apart, on greased cooky sheets. Mix ¼ cup sugar with ½ teaspoon cinnamon, and sprinkle a little on each cooky. Bake for 5 to 8 minutes, or until pale gold. (It is impossible to roll the dough to an absolutely uniform thickness; therefore, the baking time will vary.) Roll out the rest of the plain dough; cut and bake as above. Then, roll, cut, and bake the poppy seed dough, ½ at a time, but do not sprinkle with cinnamon-sugar mixture.

½ cup butter	2 cups flour
1 cup Vanilla Sugar (see Index)	1 teaspoon baking powder
	2 tablespoons poppy seeds
1 egg	¼ cup sugar
1 tablespoon cream	½ teaspoon cinnamon

YIELD: about 175 to 200 cookies

Kokosdrømme (Coconut Dreams)

The Danes know what they are talking about when they call
these coconut cookies "dreams." So they are, and easy to make,
too.

In a small saucepan, over low heat, melt 2 ounces of cocoa
butter (available at drugstores), and cool for 10 minutes. Preheat oven to 300°. Cream the cooled cocoa butter with 4 tablespoons butter and ⅓ cup sugar. Add 1 cup flour, 1½ cups
flaked coconut, and ¾ teaspoon pulverized ammonium carbonate (a leavening agent available at drugstores). Mix to a
smooth dough, shape into 30 marble-sized balls, and place, ½
inch apart, on an ungreased cooky sheet. Bake for 30 minutes.

2 ounces cocoa butter	1½ cups flaked coconut
4 tablespoons butter	¾ teaspoon pulverized ammo-
⅓ cup sugar	nium carbonate
1 cup flour	

YIELD: 30 cookies

Tosca Cookies

Preheat oven to 350°. In a bowl, mix ½ pound less 2 tablespoons butter, melted, ½ cup uncooked farina, ⅓ cup ground
almonds, 1 lightly beaten egg, ⅔ cup sugar, and 1 cup flour
sifted with 1 teaspoon baking powder. Drop rounded teaspoonfuls of the batter, 1½ inches apart, on ungreased cooky
sheet. Bake for 10 to 12 minutes until golden, remove from
oven and spread with glaze, below. Return to the oven, and
bake 5 minutes longer, or until shiny.

To make the glaze, cook 4 tablespoons butter, 6 tablespoons sugar, and ¾ tablespoon light corn syrup until the sugar dissolves. Remove from heat, and stir in ⅓ cup blanched slivered almonds.

½ pound less 2 tablespoons butter, melted
½ cup uncooked farina
⅓ cup ground almonds
1 egg
⅔ cup sugar
1 cup flour

1 teaspoon baking powder
4 tablespoons butter
6 tablespoons sugar
¾ tablespoon light corn syrup
⅓ cup blanched slivered almonds

YIELD: about 6 dozen cookies

PASTRIES

OF CREAM PUFF PASTE

Basic Cream Puff Paste

Tarte aux Profiterolles

Cream Puffs, *Salambo au Cognac*
(Cream Puffs Filled with Brandied Custard)

Veendam Puffs

Paris-Brest (Cream Puff Ring)

Sfinge di Festa (Pistachio Puffs with Cherry Custard Filling)

B.O.A.C. Pears Bristol

Cream Puff Paste (basic recipe)

In a saucepan, over medium heat, bring to a boil ¼ pound butter, cut into pieces, and 1 cup water. Add 1 cup flour, all at once, and stir vigorously until the mixture comes away from the sides of the pan and forms a ball. Turn into the small bowl of the electric mixer and add 4 eggs, one at a time, beating thoroughly, at high speed, after the addition of each egg. After the last egg is worked into the paste, beat an additional 5 minutes.

To make large Dessert Puffs, *Profiterolles*, and Éclairs, preheat oven to 375°. Through a pastry tube, fitted with a plain round opening, force out the paste onto well-greased baking sheets (or drop onto sheets from a spoon). Make 2-inch mounds for Dessert Puffs, and bake 30 to 35 minutes; ¾-inch mounds for *Profiterolles*, and bake 20 minutes; ½-by-3-inch fingers for Éclairs, and bake 25 to 30 minutes. Space the mounds 1½ inches apart on the baking sheets. To test a puff, remove from the oven; if it holds its shape, it is done. Cream Puffs freeze beautifully.

¼ pound butter
1 cup water
APPROXIMATE YIELD:

1 cup flour
4 eggs
18 Dessert Puffs or
6 dozen *Profiterolles* or
2 dozen Éclairs

Tarte aux Profiterolles

Preheat oven to 375°. Press ½ recipe Tart Dough (see Index) over the bottom and sides of an 8- or 9-inch Pyrex pie plate.

Prick surface with a fork, and bake for 12 to 15 minutes, or until pale gold. Remove from oven, and cool.

Bake ½ recipe *Profiterolles* (see Cream Puff Paste), cool, and fill the tiny puffs with ½ cup heavy cream whipped until stiff with 2 tablespoons sugar.

While the *Profiterolles* are baking, make this sauce: In a saucepan, mix 4 lightly beaten eggs with ¼ cup Vanilla Sugar (see Index). Add 4 ounces dark sweet chocolate, broken into small pieces, and 2 cups milk. Cook over low heat, stirring constantly, until the sauce thickens. Remove from heat, and cool.

Heap the filled *Profiterolles* in the baked tart shell, pour the sauce over them, scatter 2 tablespoons slivered toasted almonds over the top, and chill until servingtime.

½ recipe Tart Dough (see Index)	4 eggs
½ recipe *Profiterolles* (see Cream Puff Paste)	¼ cup Vanilla Sugar (see Index)
½ cup heavy cream	4 ounces dark sweet chocolate
2 tablespoons sugar	2 cups milk
	2 tablespoons slivered toasted almonds

YIELD: 8 servings

Cream Puffs, *Salambo au Cognac*
(Cream Puffs Filled with Brandied Custard)

Preheat oven to 375°. Prepare 1 recipe Cream Puff Paste (see Index), and force paste out in 12 extra-large mounds, instead of 18. Baking time will be 5 to 10 minutes longer. Cool.

In a saucepan, mix 6 egg yolks, ½ cup sugar, and 2 teaspoons cornstarch. Add ¾ cup cognac, and cook over low heat, stirring constantly, until mixture thickens. Remove from heat. Beat 4 egg whites until stiff but not dry, and fold into the hot custard. Refrigerate until servingtime.

Just before servingtime, make Chocolate Sauce #2 (see Index). Split puffs in half, fill with custard, and place on individual dessert plates. Pour hot sauce over puffs, and serve at once.

Cream Puff Paste (see Index)	¾ cup cognac
6 egg yolks	4 egg whites
½ cup sugar	Chocolate Sauce #2 (see
2 teaspoons cornstarch	Index)

YIELD: 12 servings

Veendam Puffs

Make 1 recipe Cream Puff Paste (see Index), spoon into a pastry tube fitted with a plain round opening, and force out 16 mounds on a greased baking sheet. Preheat oven to 375°. In a bowl, put ¼ pound sweet butter, 2 teaspoons sugar, and 1 cup flour, and, with your fingers, work to a smooth dough. Shape into a roll slightly larger than the diameter of the cream puff mounds, cut into 16 slices, and place 1 slice on top of each mound. Bake for 35 minutes, and cool.

Whip 1 pint of heavy cream until stiff with ½ cup sugar. Fold in 2 ounces of dark sweet chocolate, grated. Cut each puff in half crosswise, fill with the cream, replace top, and dust generously with confectioners' sugar.

1 recipe Cream Puff Paste (see	1 pint heavy cream
Index)	½ cup sugar
¼ pound sweet butter	2 ounces dark sweet chocolate,
2 teaspoons sugar	grated
1 cup flour	Confectioners' sugar

YIELD: 16 puffs

Paris-Brest (Cream Puff Ring)

You will notice that this recipe has a higher proportion of water than the basic Cream Puff Paste (see Index). It produces a very tender puff that is slightly moist. It was taught this way at the Cordon Bleu school in Paris.

Preheat oven to 375°. In a saucepan, over medium heat, bring 4 tablespoons butter and 1 cup water to a boil. Add ½ cup flour, all at once, and stir vigorously until the mixture comes away from the sides of the pan and forms a ball. Turn into the small bowl of the electric mixer, add 2 eggs, one at a time, beating thoroughly, at high speed, after the addition of each egg. After the second egg is worked into the paste, beat an additional 5 minutes.

On a greased baking sheet, using an 8-inch round cake pan as a guide, trace a circle. Spoon the paste into a pastry tube fitted with a plain round opening, and force out the dough within the confines of the circle, leaving a hole in the center. Brush the paste with lightly beaten egg, sprinkle with ¼ cup slivered blanched almonds, and bake for 1 hour. Cool, and split in half, crosswise.

While the puff is baking, make the filling. In a saucepan, mix ⅓ cup sugar, ¼ cup flour, 1 egg, and 2 egg yolks. Gradually add 1 cup hot milk, and stir until smooth. Cook over medium heat, stirring constantly, until the custard is thick. (Do not allow to boil.) Remove from heat, add 1 teaspoon almond extract, and cool.

Just before servingtime, beat 2 egg whites until stiff but not dry, fold into the cooled custard, and spoon into the bottom half of the puff. Cover lightly with the top, and dust generously with confectioners' sugar.

4 tablespoons butter
1 cup water
½ cup flour
2 eggs
Beaten egg
¼ cup slivered blanched
  almonds
⅓ cup sugar

¼ cup flour
1 egg
2 egg yolks
1 cup hot milk
1 teaspoon almond extract
2 egg whites
Confectioners' sugar

YIELD: 8 to 10 servings

Sfinge di Festa
(Pistachio Puffs with Cherry Custard Filling)

Preheat oven to 375°. Make 1 recipe Cream Puff Paste (see Index), and fold in ½ cup pistachio nuts, chopped. Bake 18 dessert puffs, as directed. Make 1 recipe *Crème Pâtissière* (see Index), and add ⅓ cup slivered candied cherries. Prepare 1 recipe Vanilla Sauce (see Index), cool, and fold in ¾ cup heavy cream, whipped.

Shortly before servingtime, split the puffs, and fill with the *Crème Pâtissière*-cherry mixture. Dust the puffs generously with confectioners' sugar, and pass the Vanilla Sauce separately.

1 recipe Cream Puff Paste (see
  Index)
½ cup pistachio nuts, chopped
1 recipe *Crème Pâtissière* (see
  Index)

⅓ cup slivered candied cherries
1 recipe Vanilla Sauce (see
  Index)
¾ cup heavy cream
Confectioners' sugar

YIELD: 9 servings

B.O.A.C. Pears Bristol

On a flight to Bermuda a year or so ago, a handsome dessert was served. It tasted as good as it looked, and when I returned from my holiday, I worked out the recipe.

Poach 8 medium-size pears (see Pears *à la Crème*), and chill. Preheat oven to 375°. Prepare ½ recipe of Cream Puff Paste (see Index), and bake 8 dessert puffs. Cool the puffs, and cut off the tops. Prepare 1 recipe *Crème Pâtissière* (see Index). Whip 1½ cups heavy cream until stiff with ¼ cup sugar, and chill.

An hour or less before servingtime, assemble the dessert. Fill the bottoms of the dessert puffs with *Crème Pâtissière,* and arrange the puffs, evenly spaced, on a round serving platter. Drain the pears thoroughly, and place them upright in the filled puffs. Spoon the whipped cream into a pastry tube fitted with a star-shaped opening, and pipe the cream between and all around the filled puffs. Decorate the platter with candied violets or bits of angelica. Chill until servingtime.

8 medium-size pears	1½ cups heavy cream
½ recipe Cream Puff Paste (see Index)	¼ cup sugar
	Candied violets or angelica
1 recipe *Crème Pâtissière* (see Index)	

YIELD: 8 servings

OF PUFF PASTE

————◆●◆————

Basic Puff Paste

Napoleons

St. Honoré

Tartelettes Nemours (Cream Puff Tarts)

Lucettes (Chocolate-Filled Pastries)

Schillerlocken (Lady Locks)

Palmiers (Palm Leaves)

Dartois (Almond-Filled Pastry)

Puff Paste (basic recipe)

Under very cold running water, knead and squeeze ½ pound of sweet butter, to force the moisture out of the butter. Pat the butter dry, shape into a rectangle ½ inch thick, wrap in a paper towel, and refrigerate.

Place 2 cups of flour into a bowl. Measure 2 tablespoons of chilled white wine plus enough ice water to make ⅔ cup of liquid, add to flour, and mix with the fingertips to make a dough. On a lightly floured board, roll out to a rectangle a little more than twice the size of the butter. Place butter on one half of the dough, fold over the other half, and seal edges well, and refrigerate for 20 minutes, or place in the freezer for 10 minutes.

Place dough on the board with the folded edge nearest you. Press lightly with rolling pin all over the surface of the dough, then roll out away from you in a series of quick, light, back-and-forth rolling movements, so as not to permit the butter to break through the surface of the dough. When the dough is ½ inch thick, fold the third farthest away from you toward the center, then fold the third nearest you over the other layers, making 3 layers in all. Turn the dough a quarter of the way around, so that an open edge is nearest you. Repeat the rolling and folding. Chill for 30 minutes in the refrigerator or 15 minutes in the freezer. Repeat the 2 rollings and foldings, and chill again for 30 minutes. Roll and fold twice again, and chill for 15 minutes in refrigerator. (Use as little flour on the board as possible, brushing any excess flour from dough before folding.)

The dough is now ready for use as directed under the individual recipes.

½ pound sweet butter   2 tablespoons chilled white wine
2 cups flour   Ice water

98

Napoleons

Preheat oven to 450°. On a lightly floured board, roll out Puff Paste (see opposite) to a 12-by-17-inch rectangle, ⅛ inch thick. Cut into 4 strips, 3 inches wide and 17 inches long, trim uneven edges, and reserve scraps. Place on moistened baking sheets (bake the scraps, too), and, with the tines of a fork, prick the surface of the paste.

Bake for 5 minutes, reduce heat to 375°, and bake for 20 to 25 minutes longer, or until the pastry is golden brown. (The scraps, of course, will bake a good deal sooner; don't forget to remove them.)

Spread 2 of the strips with half the Napoleon Filling (see Index), cover with remaining 2 strips, and spread remaining filling on top. Coarsely crumble the baked scraps, scatter over the top, and dust generously with confectioners' sugar.

Puff Paste (see opposite)   Confectioners' sugar
Napoleon Filling (see Index)   YIELD: 16 servings

St. Honoré

This pastry is one of the classics of the French *pâtissier*, and a handsome spectacle it is! If you don't have time to make Puff Paste for the base, use ½ recipe Tart Dough (see Index), but bake it at 375° for the whole time, about 30 minutes. I often make several *St. Honorés*, without the filling, and freeze them. (Then, I use Puff Paste.)

On a lightly floured board, roll out ½ recipe Puff Paste (see Index) ⅛ inch thick. Using a 9- or 10-inch plate or cake pan as a guide, cut out a circle. Moisten half a large baking sheet, place the circle of paste on it, prick the surface with a fork, and refrigerate.

Preheat oven to 450°. Make ½ recipe Cream Puff Paste (see Index). Through a pastry tube fitted with a plain round opening, force out about half the paste around the circumference of the Puff Paste circle. Grease the other half of the baking sheet, and force out the remaining Cream Puff Paste in ¾-inch mounds. Bake for 5 minutes, reduce heat to 375°, bake for 10 minutes longer, and remove tiny puffs. Continue baking the large shell for an additional 20 minutes, or until gold. Remove to a cake rack, and cool.

Carefully slice off the top half of the Cream Puff Paste rim and the top half of the small puffs. Fill with ⅔ cup heavy cream, whipped until stiff with 2 tablespoons sugar, and replace tops. (Or, fill small puffs through a pastry tube fitted with small round openings: Insert tip into bottom of puff, and press out whipped cream.)

In a small saucepan, over medium heat, cook ¼ cup sugar with 2 tablespoons water until the syrup caramelizes. Remove from heat, dip the bottom of the tiny puffs into the caramel, and place, tightly together, on top of the rim. (The caramel will keep the puffs in place.) Reserve leftover puffs. Fill the *St. Honoré* with Napoleon Filling (see Index), and place reserved puffs on top.

½ recipe Puff Paste (see Index)	2 tablespoons sugar
½ recipe Cream Puff Paste (see Index)	¼ cup sugar
	2 tablespoons water
⅔ cup heavy cream	Napoleon Filling (see Index)

YIELD: 12 to 16 servings

Tartelettes Nemours (Cream Puff Tarts)

Preheat oven to 375°. On a lightly floured board, roll out Puff Paste (see Index) to a square ⅛ inch thick, and divide into 24 squares. Line 2 dozen 2½-inch tart tins with the squares, and place 1 tablespoon of thick fruit jam in each.

Make ½ recipe Cream Puff Paste (see Index). Through a pastry tube fitted with a plain round opening, force paste in mounds on top of jam. (Paste will not completely cover the jam.) Bake for 35 minutes, remove from tins immediately, and set on cake racks to cool. Dust generously with confectioners' sugar.

Puff Paste (see Index)   Confectioners' sugar
1½ cups thick fruit jam
½ recipe Cream Puff Paste (see   YIELD: 24 tarts
  Index)

Lucettes (Chocolate-Filled Pastries)

Preheat oven to 450°. On a pastry board sprinkled with ½ cup sugar, and using a waffle-patterned rolling pin, roll out Puff Paste (see Index), into a rectangle a scant ⅛ inch thick. (If you do not have the patterned rolling pin, use the standard pin.) Turn paste over while rolling, to coat both sides with sugar. Cut into 48 equal-sized rectangles, place on greased baking sheets, prick with a fork, and bake for 10 minutes. Reduce heat to 375°, and bake for 8 minutes longer or until gold. Cool on cake racks. Spread half the baked pastry with Chocolate Butter Cream (see Index), and cover with the remaining pastry. If you do not plan to serve all the *Lucettes,* store those you do not use in a tightly-covered tin, and apply butter cream just prior to serving. (They will keep well in the tin for days, or in the freezer for several months.)

½ cup sugar   Chocolate Butter Cream (see
Puff Paste (see Index)   Index)
              YIELD: 24 pastries

Schillerlocken (Lady Locks)

Preheat oven to 450°. On a lightly floured board, roll out Puff Paste (see Index) to a 16-by-20-inch rectangle, and cut into 16 strips, 1 inch wide and 20 inches long. Lightly grease metal tubes (see *Cannoli*), and starting near one end of tube, wind a strip of dough around the tube, overlapping edges slightly. Roll in sugar, and bake for 10 minutes. Reduce heat to 375°, and bake about 10 minutes longer until gold. Remove from oven, gently push baked pastry off tube, and cool on cake racks.

Whip 2 cups heavy cream until stiff with ¼ cup sugar, and fill into a pastry tube fitted with plain round opening. Just before servingtime, fill Lady Locks with cream.

Puff Paste (see Index)	2 cups heavy cream
Sugar	¼ cup sugar

YIELD: 16 pastries

Palmiers (Palm Leaves)

Palmiers or Palm Leaves are known, less elegantly, as Pig's Ears or Elephant Ears, depending on size. No matter what the name, they *are* elegant and special.

Preheat oven to 450°. On a pastry board sprinkled with ¼ cup sugar, roll out Puff Paste (see Index) to a 10-by-20-inch rectangle, ¼ inch thick. Sprinkle ¼ cup sugar over the paste. Starting from the two long sides, roll each toward the center until they meet. Cut into slices ⅓ inch thick, and place, 1 inch apart, on greased baking sheets. Sprinkle with 2 tablespoons sugar. Bake for 10 minutes, reduce heat to 375°, turn

Palmiers over, and bake 10 minutes longer, or until gold. Remove to cake racks, and cool.

¼ cup sugar   ¼ cup sugar
Puff Paste (see Index)   2 tablespoons sugar
              YIELD: about 4 to 5 dozen

Dartois (Almond-Filled Pastry)

If you prefer, fill the pastry with *Crème Pâtissière* (see Index), or jam, instead of almond paste.

Preheat oven to 450°. On a lightly floured board, roll out Puff Paste (see Index) to a 7-by-15-inch rectangle. Cut into two 15-inch long strips, one 4 inches wide, and the other 3 inches wide. Make ½ recipe almond paste (see *Simnel* Cake). There will be ½ egg left over; reserve it. Spread the almond paste over the wider strip of pastry, leaving a ½-inch border all around. Bend up the border to make a low wall all around the almond filling. Moisten the top edge of the border with water, lay the other strip of pastry on top, and pinch the seam tightly together. With the tines of a fork, press lightly around the top edges. Prick the top surface with the fork. With the back of a knife blade, make 12 evenly-spaced indentations to indicate serving portions.

Place on a baking sheet moistened with water, brush the top with the reserved egg, and bake for 5 minutes. Reduce heat to 375°, and bake 25 to 30 minutes longer, or until golden brown. Cool on a cake rack. Cut into serving portions and place the slices on a platter, or slice at the table.

Puff Paste (see Index)   ½ egg
½ recipe almond paste (see   YIELD: 12 servings
   Simnel Cake)

STRUDELS

Strudel Dough (see Apfel Strudel)
Apfel Strudel (Apple Strudel)
Sour Cream Raisin Strudel
Coconut Strudel
Two-Cherry Strudel

Apfel Strudel

No two recipes for *strudel* dough seem to agree; some use egg yolk, some have butter, and some include sour cream in their composition. This one, that I worked out for myself, has as much, or more elasticity than any I have tried. It can be stretched incredibly thin, and thinness is the prerequisite of a crisp *strudel*. *Strudel* dough is not the sort of thing you make perfectly the first time, but it's worth working at, and it's fun to see a small ball of dough grow to amazing proportions as it is pulled out. Keep the dough warm; this keeps it elastic. And don't be alarmed if holes appear as you stretch the dough; that's inevitable even with the professionals.

Sift 2 cups flour and ¼ teaspoon salt onto a pastry board, and make a well in the center. In the well, pour ¾ cup plus 2 tablespoons warm water and 2 teaspoons vegetable oil. Starting from the middle, gradually blend the dry ingredients into the liquid, and work up a soft dough. With one hand, pick up the dough and crash it down on the board about a hundred times, until the dough leaves the board and the hand clean. Brush top of dough with a little oil, cover with a heated bowl, and let rest for ½ hour.

Peel 3 pounds of cooking apples. Slice thinly into a bowl, and mix with ½ cup sugar, 1 teaspoon cinnamon, and ½ cup raisins. Preheat oven to 425°. Spread a cloth or sheet over a table approximately 3 by 5 feet. Rub a little flour over the surface of the cloth.

After dough has rested, place it on the center of the cloth. Hit the dough sharply with a rolling pin, until it forms a circle about ½ inch thick. Reach under the dough, palms down, and stretch gently but quickly from the center to the outer edge. Work all around the dough until it is as thin as the membrane of an egg, though the edge will be thicker. Trim off the edge with scissors, brush the dough with ⅓ cup melted butter, and scatter with ⅓ cup fine dry bread crumbs. Cover the third of the dough nearest you with the apple filling, leaving a 2-inch border at each side uncovered. Fold borders over the apples to enclose ends. Take hold of the end of the cloth nearest you and lift it slightly. As you do so, the *strudel* will roll up away from you. Place a well-buttered baking sheet at the other end of the dough so that the last roll will deposit the *strudel* on the sheet. If the *strudel* is longer than the baking sheet, bend it into a horseshoe shape. Brush the top of the dough with 2 tablespoons melted butter, and bake for ½ hour. Leave on baking sheet and reheat in a 425° oven for 5 minutes before serving. Dust generously with confectioners' sugar.

2 cups flour	1 teaspoon cinnamon
¼ teaspoon salt	½ cup raisins
¾ cup plus 2 tablespoons warm water	⅓ cup melted butter
	⅓ cup fine dry bread crumbs
Vegetable oil	2 tablespoons melted butter
3 pounds cooking apples	Confectioners' sugar
½ cup sugar	

YIELD: 10 to 12 servings

Sour Cream Raisin *Strudel*

Almost any pie filling may be used for *strudel,* and your inventiveness can produce delectable results. Nor is *strudel* confined to dessert; filled with mushrooms or seafood, combined with just enough sauce to bind the mixture, or filled with a blend of cheeses, it makes an excellent accompaniment for cocktails.

Make dough as for *Apfel Strudel* (see above). While the dough rests, make the filling. Separate 4 eggs. To the yolks, add 2 cups sour cream, 1 cup brown sugar, 1 cup seeded raisins, and mix well. Beat the whites until stiff but not dry, and fold into yolk mixture.

Stretch dough, brush with ⅓ cup melted butter, and sprinkle with ⅓ cup fine dry bread crumbs. Spread filling, roll and bake as for *Apfel Strudel*, but decrease baking time to 15 minutes.

Dough for *Apfel Strudel* (see above)
4 eggs
2 cups sour cream
1 cup brown sugar
1 cup seeded raisins
⅓ cup melted butter
⅓ cup fine dry bread crumbs
2 tablespoons melted butter
Confectioners' sugar

YIELD: 10 to 12 servings

Coconut *Strudel*

The only difference in making Coconut or *Apfel Strudel* is the preparation of the filling and the baking time.

Make 1 recipe of *strudel* dough (see *Apfel Strudel*), and let the dough rest for ½ hour.

Make the filling: Beat 6 egg yolks with ½ cup sugar until very thick and light. Add the grated rind of 1 large lemon, 2 tablespoons lemon juice, and 1⅓ cups moist coconut. Beat 6 egg whites until stiff but not dry, and fold into the filling.

After the dough has rested, preheat oven to 425°, and stretch the dough on a cloth (see *Apfel Strudel*). Continue to follow the directions for *Apfel Strudel*, substituting the coconut filling. Bake for 15 to 20 minutes, or until gold. (Since the apples are raw, apple *strudel* requires longer baking.)

1 recipe *strudel* dough (see *Apfel Strudel*)
6 egg yolks
½ cup sugar
Grated rind of 1 large lemon
2 tablespoons lemon juice
1⅓ cups moist coconut
6 egg whites

⅓ cup melted butter (see *Apfel Strudel*)
⅓ cup fine dry bread crumbs (see *Apfel Strudel*)
2 tablespoons melted butter (see *Apfel Strudel*)
Confectioners' sugar (see *Apfel Strudel*)

YIELD: 8 to 10 servings. (Though this is the same size as *Apfel Strudel*, the filling is lighter, and will not yield as many servings.)

Two-Cherry *Strudel*

Two-Cherry *Strudel* is made and baked just like *Apfel Strudel* (see Index); the only difference is in the filling.

Make 1 recipe of *strudel* dough (see *Apfel Strudel*), and let the dough rest for ½ hour.

Make the filling: Drain two 1 pound 14 ounce cans of pitted black cherries and 3 1 pound cans of pitted light cherries in heavy syrup. To the drained cherries, add 1 cup of walnuts, chopped, ½ cup light raisins, 1 teaspoon cinnamon, and ½ cup sugar.

After the dough has rested, preheat oven to 425°, and stretch the dough on a cloth (see *Apfel Strudel*). Continue to follow the directions for *Apfel Strudel*, substituting the cherry filling.

1 recipe *strudel* dough (see *Apfel Strudel*)
2 1-pound 14-ounce cans pitted black cherries
3 1-pound cans pitted light cherries in heavy syrup
1 cup walnuts
½ cup light raisins
1 teaspoon cinnamon

½ cup sugar
⅛ cup melted butter (see *Apfel Strudel*)
⅛ cup fine dry bread crumbs (see *Apfel Strudel*)
2 tablespoons melted butter (see *Apfel Strudel*)
Confectioners' sugar (see *Apfel Strudel*)

YIELD: 10 to 12 servings

LARGE TARTS,
OPEN FRUIT CAKE

Tart Dough

Tarte aux Cerises (Cherry Meringue Tart)

Plum Tart, *la Quetsch*

Mazarintårta (Almond Tart)

Tart *Ibiza* (Lemon Tart)

Gillian's Apple Tart

Rhubarb Flan

Tarte Tatin, Oustau la Baumanière
(Upside-Down Apple Tart)

Danilovian Winter Tart

Peach *Kuchen* (Open Peach Cake)

Tart Dough

In a mixing bowl put 1⅓ cups flour, ¼ cup sugar, ½ teaspoon grated lemon rind, 2 egg yolks, and ¼ pound butter, at room temperature. (If the butter is cold, cut it into small pieces.) With your hands, work all the ingredients together until you have a smooth homogeneous dough. Use it for large or small tart shells, or, rolled a little thicker, for cookies.

1⅓ cups flour
¼ cup sugar
½ teaspoon grated lemon rind

2 egg yolks
¼ pound butter

APPROXIMATE YIELD (depending on how thick the dough is rolled or pressed into the form): Two 8- to 9-inch shells; or one 12-inch shell; or 12 to 20 small shells, according to the size of tins and thickness of dough.

Tarte aux Cerises (Cherry Meringue Tart)

Other canned fruit, or poached fresh fruit, may be substituted for the cherries. Just be sure to drain fruit well so the crust won't be soggy or the meringue too moist.

Preheat oven to 375°. Make ½ recipe Tart Dough (see the above) and press it over the bottom and sides of a scalloped 8-inch tart tin with removable bottom. (This tin makes for a very professional looking end result, but, lacking one, the same size pie plate will do.) With a fork, prick the surface of the dough at 1-inch intervals to prevent it from puffing up during baking. Bake for 12 to 15 minutes, or until pale gold. Watch it carefully toward the end. It can get too dark within a matter of seconds and this alters the fine taste.

Drain two 1-pound cans of light or dark cherries, remove pits if you have the unpitted fruit, and drain again. Turn oven heat to 500°. In the small bowl of the electric mixer, beat 4 egg whites until foamy. Gradually add ⅔ cup sugar, and continue to beat at high speed until sugar is dissolved and meringue is thick and glossy. (Meringue won't weep if the sugar is completely dissolved; adding the sugar when the whites are just foamy allows time.) Sprinkle 2 tablespoons graham cracker crumbs, or plain cooky crumbs, over the bottom of the baked tart shell. Fold the drained cherries into ⅓ of the meringue mixture, and spread over the bottom of the baked shell. Cover with remaining meringue and place in the oven for a few minutes, until the top begins to be flecked with color. Cool in the tin for ½ hour. Remove the sides of the tin by placing it on a tin can; the sides will fall to the counter. (If you have baked the tart in a regulation pie plate, serve in it as you would any pie.)

½ recipe Tart Dough (see Index)

2 1-pound cans of light or dark cherries

4 egg whites

⅔ cup sugar

2 tablespoons graham cracker crumbs or plain cooky crumbs

YIELD: 8 servings

Plum Tart, *La Quetsch*

This tart comes from the Parisian restaurant, La Quetsch, where the *patron* offers good French food served at a typical American lunch counter, and the hubbub at noon is fantastic but fun!

Press ½ recipe Tart Dough (see Index) on the bottom and sides of an 8-inch pie plate. Preheat oven to 400°. Cut 24 blue plums in half, and discard the pits. Cream 3 tablespoons butter, ¼ cup sugar, and 4 teaspoons flour. Fold in ½ cup ground almonds, and spread over the bottom of the unbaked pie shell. Arrange the plums, overlapping evenly, cut side up, in concentric circles, over the nut filling. Bake on the lowest shelf of the oven for 10 minutes. Reduce heat to 375°, and bake for 20 minutes longer. If the edge of the crust starts to get too brown, cover with strips of foil. Melt ¼ cup of currant jelly, and spread over the tart while it is still warm.

½ recipe Tart Dough (see Index)	¼ cup sugar
	4 teaspoons flour
24 blue plums	½ cup ground almonds
3 tablespoons butter	¼ cup currant jelly

YIELD: 6 servings

Mazarintårta (Almond Tart)

You can also bake this Swedish dessert in small tart shells, in which case they are called *Mazariner*. There are a few minor changes in the recipe, too: Line 16 well-greased 3-inch tart or muffin tins with a *full* recipe of Tart Dough (see Index). Preheat oven to 375°. Fill with *Mazarintårta* filling, below, and bake for 18 to 20 minutes, or until golden. Remove from tins immediately.

To make the large *tårta*, press ½ recipe Tart Dough (see Index) on the bottom and sides of an 8-inch pie plate. Preheat oven to 325°. In a bowl, cream 4 tablespoons butter with ⅔ cup sugar until light and fluffy. Add 2 egg yolks, 3 ounces of ground almonds and ¼ teaspoon almond extract. (Blanch the almonds before grinding if you prefer a yellow filling; with the skin left on, the filling will be darker. It makes no difference in the taste.) Mix well, then fold in 2 egg whites beaten until stiff but not dry. Pour into lined pie plate, and bake on the bottom shelf of the oven for 30 minutes.

½ recipe Tart Dough (see   2 egg yolks
   Index)   3 ounces ground almonds
4 tablespoons butter   ¼ teaspoon almond extract
⅔ cup sugar   2 egg whites

YIELD: 6 to 8 servings

Tart *Ibiza*

Preheat oven to 375°. Press ½ recipe Tart Dough (see Index) on the bottom and sides of an 8- or 9-inch pie plate. Prick the dough with a fork, and bake for 12 to 15 minutes, or until pale gold.

While the pie shell is baking, make the filling: In a saucepan, mix 5 egg yolks with ½ cup sugar. Add the juice of 2 lemons, ¾ cup of dry white wine, and 1 teaspoon grated orange rind. Cook over low heat, stirring constantly, for about 8 minutes, or until thick. Remove from heat, fold in 5 egg whites beaten until stiff but not dry, spoon into baked pie shell, and bake 12 minutes more.

One hour before servingtime, drain an 8-ounce can of Mandarin oranges, and pour 2 tablespoons of light rum over the fruit. At servingtime, drain the orange sections, and place all around the circumference of the pie.

½ recipe Tart Dough (see   1 teaspoon grated orange rind
   Index)   5 egg whites
5 egg yolks   1 8-ounce can Mandarin
½ cup sugar   oranges
Juice of 2 lemons   2 tablespoons light rum
¾ cup dry white wine   YIELD: 6 servings

Gillian's Apple Tart

Preheat oven to 350°. Press ½ recipe Tart Dough (see Index) on the bottom and sides of an 8- or 9-inch pie plate. In a bowl, mix ½ cup sugar, 4 egg yolks, the juice of 1 lemon, and the grated rind of ½ lemon. Peel and core 2 large apples, grate them coarsely into the bowl, and mix well. Beat 4 egg whites until they form soft peaks, gradually add ½ cup sugar, continuing to beat until thick and shiny. Fold half of this meringue into the apple mixture, pour into the pastry-lined pie plate, and bake on the bottom shelf of the oven for 25 minutes. Remove from the oven, let stand for 3 or 4 minutes, and spread the remaining meringue over the top. Sprinkle 1 tablespoon sugar over the meringue, and bake for 10 minutes longer.

½ recipe Tart Dough (see Index)	Grated rind of ½ lemon
½ cup sugar	2 large apples
4 egg yolks	4 egg whites
Juice of 1 lemon	½ cup sugar
	1 tablespoon sugar

YIELD: 6 to 8 servings

Rhubarb Flan

Preheat oven to 350°. Press ½ recipe Tart Dough (see Index) on bottom and sides of an 8-inch pie plate or loose-bottom tart tin. Slice 2 pounds of tender young rhubarb into ⅓-inch pieces, and place in unbaked crust. In a bowl, mix 2 lightly beaten eggs, 2 tablespoons flour, ½ cup sugar, ½ teaspoon vanilla, and 2 cups of light cream. Pour over the rhubarb, and bake on the bottom shelf of the oven for 40 minutes, or until the custard is set. At servingtime, dust with confectioners' sugar. (If you use a tart tin, remove the tart to a platter before serving.)

½ recipe Tart Dough (see Index)

2 pounds tender young rhubarb

2 eggs

2 tablespoons flour

½ cup sugar

½ teaspoon vanilla

2 cups light cream

Confectioners' sugar

YIELD: 6 servings

Tarte Tatin, Oustau la Baumanière
(Upside-Down Apple Tart)

Upside-down apple tart is another specialty of this three-star restaurant. (See *Petits Soufflés a l'Orange*.) In France, the *Guide Michelin* rates restaurants on cuisine, service, etc. Only a handful are deemed worthy of the highest accolade, three-stars. *Oustau la Baumanière* is one of them.

Preheat oven to 425°. Spread ½ cup butter on the bottom of an 11-inch pie plate. Sprinkle with ½ cup sugar. Peel and core 12 medium-size Golden Delicious apples. Cut in eighths, and heap into the pie plate. Between 2 sheets of waxed paper, roll out 1 recipe Tart Dough (see Index) to a circle large enough to cover the apples. Peel off the top piece of paper, invert over the apples, and peel off the other piece of paper. (If the dough is too soft after rolling to peel off the paper easily, place in refrigerator for a little while.) Bake for 45 minutes. If the crust starts to get too brown, cover lightly with a piece of foil. Remove pie from oven, and let stand for 5 minutes. Preheat broiler. Invert pie onto a large ovenproof platter, sprinkle the top with ⅓ cup sugar, and place under broiler, 2 or 3 inches from heat, until sugar caramelizes. Remove from broiler, sprinkle with an additional ⅓ cup sugar, and set under heat to caramelize again.

Serve *Tarte Tatin* slightly warm. Whip 1 cup heavy cream slightly, pour into a bowl, and pass separately.

½ cup butter	⅓ cup sugar
½ cup sugar	⅓ cup sugar
12 medium-size Golden Delicious apples	1 cup heavy cream
1 recipe Tart Dough (see Index)	

YIELD: 12 servings

Danilovian Winter Tart

Very often I combine two, or even three, fruits in this tart.

Preheat oven to 350°. Press 1 recipe Tart Dough (see Index) on the bottom and 1 inch up the sides of a 9-inch spring-form pan. Prick the dough with a fork, and bake for 20 to 25 minutes, or until pale gold. Remove from the oven and cool.

Spread 3 cups of very well-drained stewed or canned fruit over the cooled crust. Reduce oven heat to 325°. Beat 4 egg yolks with ¾ cup sugar until thick and light. Fold in ¾ cup ground almonds or walnuts, then 4 egg whites beaten until stiff but not dry. Pour over the fruit, sprinkle the top with 1 tablespoon sugar, and bake for 25 minutes. Cool in the pan, remove sides of pan, and place cake (still on the bottom of the pan) on a platter.

1 recipe Tart Dough (see Index)	¾ cup sugar
3 cups of well-drained stewed or canned fruit	¾ cup ground almonds or walnuts
4 egg yolks	4 egg whites
	1 tablespoon sugar

YIELD: 8 servings

Peach *Kuchen* (Open Peach Cake)

Preheat oven to 400°. Sift together 1½ cups flour, 2 teaspoons baking powder, and ¼ cup sugar. Cut in 4 tablespoons butter until the mixture forms crumbs. Mix 1 lightly beaten egg, 1 teaspoon vanilla, and ⅓ cup milk, and stir into the crumb mixture until it is well blended. Spoon the dough into a well-greased 8-inch-square pan. Pit 5 to 6 medium-size peaches, cut into quarters, and place the fruit, cut side up, on the dough. (Arrange the fruit very close together and in straight rows.) Mix ⅓ cup sugar, 1½ tablespoons flour, and ½ teaspoon cinnamon, and sprinkle over the fruit. Lightly beat 1 egg yolk with 2 tablespoons heavy cream, and dribble over the surface. Loosely cover the pan with aluminum foil, and bake for 15 minutes. Remove the foil, and bake 20 minutes longer, or until the cake starts to shrink from the sides of the pan. Serve the cake slightly warm.

1½ cups flour
2 teaspoons baking powder
¼ cup sugar
4 tablespoons butter
1 lightly beaten egg
1 teaspoon vanilla
⅓ cup milk

5 to 6 medium-size peaches
⅓ cup sugar
1½ tablespoons flour
½ teaspoon cinnamon
1 egg yolk
2 tablespoons heavy cream

YIELD: 6 to 8 servings

CRÊPES

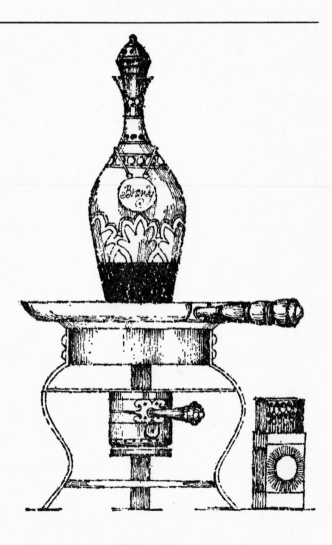

CRÊPES

Basic *Crêpes*

Crêpes Flambées Limousin (*Crêpes* in Brandy Sauce)

Crêpes Saint Marin (*Crêpes* filled with Rice *Soufflé*)

Empress *Crêpes*

Pudding *Gitane* (Gypsy Pudding)

Crêpes Bruxelloise (*Crêpes* with Ice Cream)

Topfenpalatschinken (Cottage Cheese Pancakes)

Pannequets Vert-Galant (*Soufflé* in a *Crêpe*)

Palacsinta under a Cloud
(Layered *Crêpes*, Meringue Topping)

Crêpes Rothschild

Basic *Crêpes*

Sift together ½ cup flour and ½ tablespoon sugar. Beat 2 eggs, preferably with a whisk, add dry ingredients, and beat again. (A French wire whisk makes lumps disappear like magic.) Gradually pour in ½ cup milk and ½ cup water, and continue beating until batter is smooth.

Over high heat, heat a heavy 6- to 7-inch frying pan until a speck of butter sizzles at the touch of it. Brush bottom of pan with just enough butter to coat it, ladle about 2 tablespoons of batter into pan, tilting it so that batter covers bottom. Fry until slightly brown on bottom and dry on top. Turn with a spatula, fry other side for 20 to 30 seconds, and tip out onto a plate. Repeat until batter is used up.

½ cup flour	½ cup milk
½ tablespoon sugar	½ cup water
2 eggs	Butter for frying

YIELD: about 12 *crêpes*

Crêpes Flambées Limousin
(*Crêpes* in Brandy Sauce)

Sift together ¾ cup flour, ¼ cup cocoa and 2 tablespoons sugar. Beat 4 eggs, preferably with a whisk, add dry ingredients, and beat again. Gradually pour in 1 cup milk and 1 cup water, and continue beating until batter is smooth. (Using a whisk will practically guarantee a smooth batter, free of lumps.)

Over high heat, heat a heavy 6- or 7-inch frying pan until a speck of butter sizzles at the touch of it. Dip a pastry brush in

softened butter, and brush bottom of pan with just enough
butter to coat it. Ladle about 2 tablespoons of batter into pan,
tilting it so that batter covers bottom. Fry over high heat until
slightly brown on bottom and dry on top. Turn with a spatula,
fry other side for 20 or 30 seconds, and tip out onto a plate.
Repeat until there are 24 *crêpes*.

Crumble 8 almond macaroons, sprinkle with ¼ cup *crème
de cacao* and mash to a paste. Put a little of this mixture on
each *crêpe* and fold in half lengthwise, then in half crosswise,
to make 24 wedge-shaped pieces. In a large frying pan or
chafing dish, melt 2 tablespoons butter. Add 2 tablespoons
sugar, 1 tablespoon grated orange rind, and ¾ cup *fine champagne* or cognac. Over medium heat, stir until sugar is dissolved. Whip 1 cup heavy cream until stiff with 3 tablespoons
sugar, and chill. (Preparation up to this point may be done in
advance.)

At servingtime, reheat brandy syrup, place the *crêpes* in the
pan, turn them to coat both sides with syrup, and simmer until
crêpes are hot. Heat ¼ cup *fine champagne* or cognac, ignite,
and pour flaming over the *crêpes*. Pass bowl of whipped cream
separately.

¾ cup flour	2 tablespoons butter
¼ cup cocoa	2 tablespoons sugar
2 tablespoons sugar	1 tablespoon grated orange rind
4 eggs	¾ cup *fine champagne* or
1 cup milk	cognac
1 cup water	1 cup heavy cream
Butter for frying	3 tablespoons sugar
8 almond macaroons	¼ cup *fine champagne* or
¼ cup *crème de cacao*	cognac

YIELD: 8 servings

Crêpes Saint Marin
(*Crêpes* Filled with Rice *Soufflé*)

In a saucepan, over medium heat, bring to a boil 4 tablespoons rice, ⅛ teaspoon salt, ¼ cup sugar, and 1¼ cups milk. Cover pot, turn heat low, and simmer for 30 minutes, or until rice is tender and liquid almost absorbed. Remove from heat, stir in 2 tablespoons heavy cream, ¼ cup minced, candied fruits, and 2 egg yolks.

While the rice is cooking, make the Basic *Crêpes* (see Index). Preparation to this point may be done in advance.

Shortly before servingtime, preheat oven to 400°. Beat 2 egg whites until stiff, fold into the rice mixture, and spoon a portion of it down the center of each *crêpe*. Roll *crêpes* loosely and place in a single layer in a buttered shallow baking dish. Bake for 7 minutes. While *crêpes* are in the oven, whip ¾ cup heavy cream until stiff with 4 tablespoons sugar. Remove the *crêpes* from the oven, dust with confectioners' sugar, and serve immediately. Pass the bowl of whipped cream separately.

1 recipe Basic *Crêpes* (see Index)	¼ cup candied fruits, minced
4 tablespoons rice	2 egg yolks
⅛ teaspoon salt	2 egg whites
¼ cup sugar	¾ cup heavy cream
1¼ cups milk	4 tablespoons sugar
2 tablespoons heavy cream	Confectioners' sugar

YIELD: **6** servings

Empress *Crêpes*

Make Basic *Crêpes* (see Index). (*Crêpes* may be made in advance and even frozen, stacked with a piece of foil between each. They take but a little while to defrost.)

Mix ½ cup ground walnuts with ½ cup apricot jam, and spread some of this mixture on each *crêpe*. Fold each *crêpe* in half, then in half again (the shape will be ¼ of a circle). Refrigerate filled *crêpes* until ready to use.

In a chafing dish, over direct heat, melt 4 tablespoons butter. Add ¼ cup sugar, ¼ cup orange juice, and ½ cup apricot jam, and bring to a boil. Place each of the filled *crêpes* in the hot syrup, turn over to coat both sides with syrup, and simmer until *crêpes* are very hot. Remove chafing dish to a trivet for a moment. Pour ¼ cup Benedictine into a small saucepan, and hold over heat until Benedictine is warm. Replace chafing dish, ignite Benedictine, and pour, flaming, over *crêpes*.

1 recipe Basic *Crêpes* (see Index)	¼ cup sugar
	¼ cup orange juice
½ cup ground walnuts	½ cup apricot jam
½ cup apricot jam	¼ cup Benedictine
4 tablespoons butter	YIELD: 4 to 6 servings

Pudding *Gitane* (Gypsy Pudding)

Plump ¼ cup seeded raisins in hot water for 15 minutes, and drain. Peel, core, and dice 2 pounds of cooking apples. In a covered saucepan, over low heat, cook the apples with ¼ cup water until tender. Remove from heat, mash with a fork, and add ½ teaspoon grated lemon rind, the drained raisins, ⅛ teaspoon cinnamon, and sugar to taste.

Make 1 recipe Basic *Crêpes* (see Index), place a spoonful of the apple filling in the center of each *crêpe*, and fold to enclose filling.

Preheat oven to 350°. In a saucepan, beat 4 eggs, ½ cup Vanilla Sugar (see Index), and ⅛ teaspoon salt. Add 2 cups milk, and cook over low heat, stirring constantly, until custard coats the spoon. Remove from heat. In a deep 8-inch baking dish, alternate layers of custard and filled *crêpes*, starting and ending with custard. Place the dish in a pan of hot water, and bake for 40 to 45 minutes, or until a knife blade inserted 1 inch from the edge comes out clean. Remove from oven, and serve with Wine *Chaudeau* (see Index), Rum Sauce (see Index), or Brandied Fruit Sauce (see Index).

Pudding *Gitane* may be made in advance and reheated. Cover top with foil, set in a pan of hot water, and reheat in a 350° oven.

¼ cup seeded raisins
2 pounds cooking apples
¼ cup water
½ teaspoon grated lemon rind
⅛ teaspoon cinnamon
Sugar to taste
1 recipe Basic *Crêpes* (see Index)
4 eggs

½ cup Vanilla Sugar (see Index)
⅛ teaspoon salt
2 cups milk
Wine *Chaudeau* (see Index) or Rum Sauce (see Index) Brandied Fruit Sauce (see Index)

YIELD: 8 servings

Crêpes Bruxelloise (Crêpes with Ice Cream)

Make 1 recipe Basic *Crêpes* (see Index). In a large chafing dish, over direct heat, melt 4 tablespoons butter. Add ½ cup sugar, and cook for 1 minute. Add 1 cup light rum, heat until the rum is warm, and ignite. After the flames have died out, bathe 12 *crêpes*, one at a time, in the syrup, and stack them on one side of the pan.

Working quickly, place a *crêpe* on a dessert plate, top it with a scoop of vanilla or coffee ice cream, cover it with another *crêpe*, spoon a little of the syrup on top, and scatter 1 tablespoon of slivered toasted almonds overall. Repeat with remaining *crêpes*.

1 recipe Basic *Crêpes* (see Index)	1 quart vanilla or coffee ice cream
4 tablespoons butter	6 tablespoons slivered toasted almonds
½ cup sugar	
1 cup light rum	

YIELD: 6 servings

Topfenpalatschinken (Cottage Cheese Pancakes)

The advice of a young Austrian music student led me to the *bierstube* of one of the large hotels in Salzburg. I had been told to order these cheese-filled *crêpes*. After lunch, I waited until the chef was free; I couldn't come home without *that* recipe!

With 1 recipe of Basic *Crêpes* batter (see Index), make 12 *crêpes*. Preheat oven to 500°. In an electric blender, whirl until smooth: 3 slices of white bread, ⅔ cup milk, 6 egg yolks, ⅔ cup sugar, ¼ pound butter, 1 pound cottage cheese, 1 teaspoon vanilla, and the grated rind of 1 lemon. (To get the mixture smooth enough, a blender is a must. If your blender is small, whirl half the ingredients at a time.) Pour into a bowl, stir in ½ cup currants, and fold in 6 stiffly beaten egg whites. Put a large spoonful of the mixture down the center of each *crêpe*, roll loosely, and place the filled *crêpes*, side by side and seam-side down, in a large shallow baking dish. Pour the remaining filling over the *crêpes*, and bake for 4 to 5 minutes, or until a light film forms on top. Do not overbake; the filling must remain creamy.

If you have a freezer, you may prepare the dish, ready for baking, 1 hour ahead of time, and set in the freezer until baking time.

1 recipe Basic *Crêpes* (see Index)	¼ pound butter
	1 pound cottage cheese
3 slices white bread	1 teaspoon vanilla
⅔ cup milk	Grated rind of 1 lemon
6 egg yolks	½ cup currants
⅔ cup sugar	6 egg whites

YIELD: 12 servings

Pannequets Vert-Galant (Soufflé in a Crêpe)

At the restaurant Le Vert-Galant, in Paris, one of the specialties is a large *crêpe* filled with *soufflé*.

With the batter of 1 recipe Basic *Crêpes* (see Index), make 6 large *crêpes*. (Use a scant ⅓ cup batter for each *crêpe*, and fry in a 9-inch pan.) In a saucepan, mix 6 tablespoons flour, 6 tablespoons Vanilla Sugar (see Index), and ⅓ teaspoon salt. Gradually add 1½ cups milk. Cook over low heat, stirring constantly, until thick. Remove from heat, add 6 egg yolks, and replace over heat for a minute or so, still stirring vigorously, until the mixture is at the boiling point. (But, do not allow it to boil.) Remove from heat, and set aside. (Preparation up to this point may be done in advance.)

Twenty minutes before servingtime, preheat oven to 400°. Beat 6 egg whites until stiff but not dry, and fold into the custard. Spoon a portion of this soufflé mixture down the center of each *crêpe*. Roll the *crêpes* very loosely, and place them, seam-side down, on a buttered baking sheet. Bake for 7 or 8 minutes. (The *soufflé* must remain very creamy, and the *crêpe* must not dry out.) With the aid of 2 pancake turners or broad spatulas, carefully transfer the *pannequets* to individual dessert plates. Dust with confectioners' sugar, and serve immediately. Pass a bottle of Grand Marnier, so that each guest may pour some over his *pannequet*.

(If you have a freezer, you may prepare the dish, ready for baking, 1 hour ahead of time, and set in the freezer until bakingtime. You may have to bake it a minute longer to compensate for chilling in the freezer.)

1 recipe Basic *Crêpes* batter (see Index)	1½ cups milk
6 tablespoons flour	6 egg yolks
6 tablespoons Vanilla Sugar (see Index)	6 egg whites
⅓ teaspoon salt	Confectioners' sugar
	Grand Marnier

YIELD: 6 servings

Palacsinta under a Cloud
(Layered *Crêpes*, Meringue Topping)

The Hungarians have devised many desserts featuring their tissue-thin pancakes; this is a particularly festive one.

Make 1½ recipes Basic *Crêpes* (see Index). Coarsely grate 4 ounces of semisweet chocolate. In a buttered 9-inch pie plate that can come to the table, stack the *crêpes*, sprinkling some of the chocolate on each layer. (Preparation up to this point may be done in advance.)

Twenty-five minutes before servingtime, preheat oven to 325°. Beat 3 egg whites until they form moist peaks, gradually add ½ cup sugar, continuing to beat until thick and shiny. Spread the meringue over the top and sides of the *crêpes*, and bake for 12 minutes. Serve immediately, cut in wedges.

If you have a freezer, you may prepare the dish ready for baking 1 hour ahead of time, and set in the freezer until bakingtime.

1½ recipes Basic *Crêpes* (see Index)	3 egg whites
	½ cup sugar
4 ounces semisweet chocolate	

YIELD: 8 servings

Crêpes Rothschild

The Parisian restaurant, La Quetsch, furnished this recipe. The beauty of it is that it can be prepared beforehand, yet it's an elegant company dessert.

Marinate ⅓ cup candied fruits, finely minced, in 2 table-spoons kirsch for 1 hour. Prepare 1 recipe of Basic *Crêpes* (see Index), and a double recipe of *Crème Pâtissière* (see Index). Mix the *crème* with the fruits and their marinade, and spoon a portion of the mixture down the center of each *crêpe*. (You should have 12 to 14 *crêpes*.) Roll up the *crêpes*, and place them, seam-side down and in a single layer, in a buttered, shallow, ovenproof dish that can come to the table. (Preparation up to this point may be done in advance.)

Twenty minutes before servingtime, preheat oven to 500°. Just before serving, place *crêpes* in the oven for 4 minutes, or until heated through. Dust generously with Confectioners' sugar, and serve immediately.

⅓ cup candied fruits, finely minced
2 tablespoons kirsch
1 recipe Basic *Crêpes* (see Index)

Double recipe *Crème Pâtissière* (see Index)
Confectioners' sugar

YIELD: 6 to 7 servings

PANCAKES,
OMELETTES, ROULADES

PANCAKES, OMELETTES, ROULADES

Kiraly Kenyér (Hungarian Bread Dessert)

Apfel Pfannenkuchen (Apple Pancake)

Marillen Roulade (Apricot Roll)

Clafoutis aux Pruneaux (Baked Prune Pancake)

Clafoutis Limousin (Baked Cherry Pancake—see *Clafoutis aux Pruneaux*)

Matzoth Brie (Matzoth Pancake)

Omelette Surprise

Omelettes George Sand (Chocolate *Omelettes*)

Kaiserschmarren (Kaiser's Pancake)

Király Kenyér (Hungarian Bread Dessert)

This Hungarian bread dessert is of peasant origin, simple and easy to make, and perfect to top off a soup-and-salad supper; or, served with fruit conserve and sour cream, a good luncheon dish. A delicious ending for stale bread or bits of coffee cake.

Cut 10 slices of firm-textured white bread into ½-inch squares. Put into a large bowl. Beat 6 eggs with ½ cup Vanilla Sugar (see Index), add 1 quart milk, and stir to blend. Pour over bread, add ¼ cup Sultana raisins, and mix thoroughly.

In a Dutch oven or heavy pan, over medium heat, melt 4 tablespoons butter. Pour in bread mixture, cover pan, and cook for 30 minutes, turning the mixture frequently with a spatula. Uncover pan, turn up heat, and cook a few minutes longer, until liquid evaporates and bottom and sides are slightly crisp.

Serve on individual plates, crisp side up. Dust generously with Vanilla Confectioners' Sugar (see Index).

10 slices firm-textured white bread	1 quart milk
6 eggs	¼ cup Sultana raisins
½ cup Vanilla Sugar (see Index)	4 tablespoons butter
	Confectioners' Vanilla Sugar (see Index)

YIELD: 8 servings

Apfel Pfannenkuchen (Apple Pancake)

All the preparation for this apple pancake, up to the final broiling, may be done hours ahead. Make a batter by beating 2 eggs, 1 tablespoon sugar, and ½ cup flour. Gradually add ½ cup milk and ½ cup water, and continue beating, preferably with a whisk, until the batter is smooth. Let the batter stand for 1 hour. Peel and core 2 medium-size apples, and chop coarsely. In a large heavy frying pan, over medium heat, sauté the apples in 3 tablespoons of butter until tender and golden brown. Remove apples and set aside.

In a 9-inch heavy pan, over low heat, melt 1 tablespoon butter. Distribute half the chopped apples evenly over the bottom of the pan, pour in half the batter, and cook until the underside is golden and the top dry. With the aid of a broad spatula, slide out, fried side down, onto a large buttered baking sheet. Repeat with remaining apples and batter. Mix ¼ cup sugar with ½ teaspoon cinnamon, and sprinkle over the pancakes.

Fifteen minutes before servingtime, preheat the broiler. Five minutes before servingtime, pour ¼ cup of melted butter over the pancakes, and broil until the top is brown and bubbling.

Instead of two 9-inch pancakes, you may make 4 individual pancakes in a 6- to 7-inch pan, or 1 large pancake in a 12-inch pan. (Broil the large pancake in the pan in which it cooked on top of the stove; it is not necessary to transfer it to a baking sheet.)

Apfel Pfannenkuchen is also an excellent main course for luncheon.

2 eggs	3 tablespoons butter
1 tablespoon sugar	2 tablespoons butter
½ cup flour	¼ cup sugar
½ cup milk	½ teaspoon cinnamon
½ cup water	¼ cup melted butter
2 medium-size apples	

YIELD: 4 dessert servings or 2 luncheon servings

Marillen Roulade (Apricot Roll)

Preheat oven to 325°. In a saucepan, over low heat, melt 4 tablespoons butter. Add ½ cup flour, and stir with a whisk until smooth and bubbling. Gradually add 2 cups of hot milk, and cook, stirring constantly, until the sauce is thick. Remove from heat, add ⅓ cup sugar and 4 egg yolks, and mix well. Beat 4 egg whites until stiff but not dry, and fold into the yolk mixture. Grease a 10-by-15-inch jelly-roll pan, line with waxed paper, grease the paper generously, and dust with 3 tablespoons sugar. Pour the batter into the pan, spread evenly, and bake for 40 minutes, or until the top is lightly flecked with gold.

Working rapidly, sprinkle 2 tablespoons of sugar over the surface, cover the pan with a sheet of waxed paper a little longer than the pan, and invert the pan onto a board. Remove pan, and peel off the paper that is now on top. (If the paper sticks in spots use the tip of a sharp knife to loosen it from the *roulade*.) Spread with filling, below, and, starting from the long side of the *roulade*, roll it up so that the last turn deposits it onto a heated serving platter. (To facilitate rolling, grasp the waxed paper at the end nearest you, and lift slightly; as you lift, the *roulade* will roll up very easily.) Serve immediately with Rum Sauce (see Index) or Chocolate Sauce #2 (see Index), passed separately.

While the *roulade* is baking, make the filling: Simmer 10 dried apricot halves in water to cover until tender. Drain, chop coarsely, and mix with ¾ cup apricot jam.

If you plan the *roulade* as dessert for dinner, it is more convenient to finish it just before you sit down. Place it in a shallow ovenproof dish that can go to the table, cover with foil, and keep it hot in a 200° oven. Or, you may finish it hours ahead, transfer it to the shallow ovenproof dish, cover with foil, and reheat it in a 325° oven for 20 to 25 minutes, or until heated through.

4 tablespoons butter	2 tablespoons sugar
½ cup flour	Rum Sauce (see Index) or
2 cups hot milk	Chocolate Sauce #2 (see
⅓ cup sugar	Index)
4 egg yolks	10 dried apricot halves
4 egg whites	¾ cup apricot jam
3 tablespoons sugar	

YIELD: 8 servings

Clafoutis aux Pruneaux (Baked Prune Pancake)

Categorically speaking, you might dispute my listing *Clafoutis* with pancakes and omelettes, and, depending upon the recipe you have in mind, you might be right. This is a hearty peasant dish, of which there are many variations. Some recipes stipulate that *Clafoutis* be baked in a crust; some call for a very heavy, floury batter, and others for a very liquid one. Some suggest that it be eaten cold; others say hot or warm. The best known, and probably original, recipe was *Clafoutis Limousin.* You may substitute 48 large, pitted black cherries for the prunes. Fresh cherries are preferable, and do not cook them, as you do the prunes.

Simmer 12 large prunes in water to cover until just tender. Drain, remove the pits, and cut in quarters. Preheat oven to 400°. Place the fruit, evenly spaced, in a well-buttered 9- or 10-inch pie plate. Make a batter by beating 2 eggs with ¼ cup sugar, ¼ cup flour, and ⅛ teaspoon baking powder. Gradually add 1⅓ cups milk and 2 tablespoons sour cream, and beat until smooth. Pour over the prunes. Sprinkle 1 tablespoon sugar over the top, and bake for 45 minutes, or until the top is golden. Dust generously with confectioners' sugar, and serve hot.

12 large prunes	1⅓ cups milk
2 eggs	2 tablespoons sour cream
¼ cup sugar	1 tablespoon sugar
¼ cup flour	Confectioners' sugar
⅛ teaspoon baking powder	

YIELD: 4 to 6 servings

Matzoth Brie (Matzoth Pancake)

I have often served this hearty Middle European pancake as a main course for lunch, or as dessert following a light meal.

Place 12 round tea matzoths in a large bowl, cover with hot water, and soak for 5 minutes. Drain in a colander, and press out all the water. In the bowl, beat 8 eggs until light. Add ½ teaspoon salt, 3 tablespoons sugar, 1 teaspoon cinnamon, 1 teaspoon vanilla, ⅓ cup raisins, and 2 cooking apples, peeled and coarsely grated. Add the matzoths, and, with a fork, blend the mixture lightly but thoroughly.

Over low heat, heat a large heavy frying pan or griddle. Melt enough butter to coat the bottom lightly, and ladle in the batter to form pancakes 5 inches in diameter and ½ inch thick. Fry until golden on the bottom, turn and fry the other side, adding more butter as required. (If you cannot fry all the pancakes at once, preheat the oven to 250°, place the finished pancakes on a baking sheet, and keep hot in the oven.) Serve immediately, with a shaker of cinnamon and sugar and a bowl of sour cream, passed separately.

12 round tea matzoths
8 eggs
½ teaspoon salt
3 tablespoons sugar
1 teaspoon cinnamon
1 teaspoon vanilla

⅓ cup raisins
2 cooking apples, peeled and
       coarsely grated
Butter for frying
Cinnamon and sugar
Sour cream

YIELD: 8 to 10 servings

Omelette Surprise

Preheat oven to 350°. In a bowl, beat 2 eggs with 1 teaspoon of water until well blended but not frothy. Over medium heat, heat an *omelette* pan or heavy iron frying pan. (To test the heat, take a bit of butter on the end of a fork and put it in the pan; it should sizzle, but not brown. With a paper towel, wipe off the test butter before proceeding with the *omelette*.) Melt 1 tablespoon butter, and pour in the eggs. With the flat of a fork, stir the eggs rapidly, meanwhile shaking the pan back and forth with the left hand to keep the *omelette* loose. When the eggs are set on the bottom but still creamy on top, spoon 2 tablespoons of strawberry jam down the center of the *omelette*. With the aid of the fork, roll the *omelette*, and tip out onto a plate.

Make another *omelette* of 4 eggs: In a bowl, beat 4 eggs with 2 teaspoons water until well blended but not frothy. To the beaten eggs, add 4 almond macaroons, crumbled, and 3 tablespoons candied fruits, very finely minced. Cook the *omelette* as above, but instead of the jam, place the first *omelette* on the center of this *omelette*, before rolling it up. Tip out onto a buttered, shallow baking dish.

Beat 2 egg yolks with ¼ cup sugar until thick and light. Fold in 2 stiffly beaten egg whites, spread over the *omelette*, and sprinkled with 1 tablespoon sugar. Bake for 15 minutes, and serve immediately.

2 eggs	3 tablespoons candied fruits,
1 teaspoon water	very finely minced
Butter for frying	2 egg yolks
2 tablespoons strawberry jam	¼ cup sugar
4 eggs	2 egg whites
2 teaspoons water	1 tablespoon sugar
4 almond macaroons	YIELD: 5 to 6 servings

Omelettes George Sand (Chocolate *Omelettes*)

When you make these individual *omelettes* in quantity, it is more practical to make them in advance, and reheat them. Otherwise the first few are cold by the time the last one is done.

In a saucepan, over low heat, stirring constantly, heat ¾ pound semisweet chocolate with 1½ cups each of sugar and cream, until the chocolate is melted. Lightly beat 12 egg yolks, add half the chocolate sauce, and fold in 12 egg whites, stiffly beaten.

Heat a 5- to 6-inch heavy frying pan over low heat, melt 1 teaspoon of butter, and pour in a portion of the batter (about ¾ cup). Gently pull in the edges of the *omelette* with a spoon, and spread some of the uncooked surface to the edge. (Pay strict attention to the heat, since chocolate burns easily; if the *omelette* starts to scorch, reduce the heat immediately.) When the *omelette* is set at the bottom but still very moist and creamy on top, fold in half, and tip out into a large, buttered, shallow baking dish, that can go to the table. Repeat with remaining batter. (You will have 10 to 12 *omelettes*; 2 large dishes will probably be needed. Or, place each *omelette* in an individual shallow baking dish.)

Fifteen minutes before servingtime, preheat oven to 425°. Warm the remaining chocolate sauce. Place the *omelettes* in the oven for 5 minutes, or until heated through. Spoon a little of the sauce over the *omelettes,* and serve immediately. Pass the remainder of the sauce in a sauceboat.

¾ pound semisweet chocolate
1½ cups sugar
1½ cups cream
12 egg yolks

12 egg whites
About 4 tablespoons butter for frying
YIELD: 10 to 12 servings

Kaiserschmarren (Kaiser's Pancake)

In a mixing bowl, beat 4 egg yolks with 2 cups of milk, until blended. Add 1½ cups flour, and ¼ teaspoon salt, and stir until smooth. Fold in 4 egg whites, beaten until stiff but not dry.

Over medium heat, melt 1 tablespoon butter in a heavy 7-inch frying pan. Pour in ⅙ of the batter, sprinkle 2 tablespoons of raisins over the batter, and fry until the underside of the pancake is pale gold. Turn, and fry the other side until pale gold; then, with 2 forks, tear the pancake into bite-size pieces. Transfer to a baking sheet set over a pot of simmering water, and cover the cooked pancake loosely with a piece of foil. Repeat with remaining batter.

To serve, remove the pancakes to a serving platter or 6 dessert plates, and dust with ¼ cup Vanilla Sugar (see Index).

4 egg yolks
2 cups milk
1½ cups flour
¼ teaspoon salt
4 egg whites

6 tablespoons butter
¾ cup raisins
¼ cup Vanilla Sugar (see Index)
YIELD: 6 servings

BEIGNETS, FRITTERS, DUMPLINGS

BEIGNETS, FRITTERS, DUMPLINGS

———◆◆———

Beignets à la Dijonnaise (Meringue Fritters)

Dattes Marivaux (Date Fritters)

Schlosserbuben (Prune Fritters)

Hjortetak (Norwegian Doughnuts)

Gretel's *Arme Ritter* (Rolled French Toast)

Bignè di Ricotta (Deep-Fried Cheese Puffs)

Crème Frite Marianne (Fried Cream Croquettes)

Eva's *Zwetschkenknödel* (Plum Dumplings)

Cannoli (Filled Deep-Fried Pastries)

Beignets à la Dijonnaise (Meringue Fritters)

First, make small Meringues: Preheat oven to 250°. Beat 2 egg whites until they form moist peaks. Gradually add ½ cup sugar, beating all the while, and continue beating until the sugar is dissolved and the mixture thick and glossy. Spoon meringue mixture into a pastry tube or bag fitted with a plain round opening, and pipe 24 one-inch rounds, spaced 1½ inches apart, on buttered cooky sheets. (You may do without the tube and just place heaping teaspoonfuls of the meringue mixture on buttered sheets. However, I find it easier and quicker with a pastry bag, and the Meringues are even and smooth, though in this case appearance doesn't matter because they are dipped in batter and fried.)

Bake for 20 minutes, turn off heat, and leave in oven 1 hour to dry. With the point of a sharp knife make a small depression in the bottom of each Meringue. Fill with ½ teaspoon of black currant jam (or other thick flavorful jam), and put together in pairs.

An hour before servingtime, make a batter by beating 1 egg with ½ cup flour, gradually add ⅓ cup milk, and beat until smooth. At servingtime, dip Meringues in batter and fry in deep fat at 375°. Drain on absorbent paper, dust generously with confectioners' sugar, and serve immediately.

2 egg whites	½ cup flour
½ cup sugar	⅓ cup milk
Black currant jam	Deep fat for frying
1 egg	Confectioners' sugar

YIELD: 12 *beignets*

Dattes Marivaux (Date Fritters)

Make ½ recipe milk rice for Bananas *con Arroz* (see Index), substituting Cointreau for sweet sherry. Pit 36 extra large dates and fill cavity with 1 teaspoon rice mixture.

An hour before servingtime, make a double recipe of batter for *Beignets à la Dijonnaise* (see Index). At servingtime, dip dates in batter and fry in deep fat at 370°. Drain on absorbent paper, dust generously with powdered sugar, and serve immediately.

½ recipe milk rice for Bananas *con Arroz* (see Index)	Double recipe of batter for *Beignets à la Dijonnaise* (see above)
1 tablespoon Cointreau	
36 extra large dates	Deep fat for frying
Powdered sugar	YIELD: 6 servings

Schlosserbuben (Prune Fritters)

Put 12 large prunes in a saucepan. Pour in water to cover and soak for 1 hour. Cook over medium heat until the prunes are tender. Drain, and cool. Remove pits and replace with 12 blanched almonds.

An hour before servingtime make the batter for *Beignets à la Dijonnaise* (see Index). At servingtime, dip prunes in batter and fry in deep fat at 370°. Drain on absorbent paper, and roll in a mixture of 1½ ounces semisweet chocolate, grated, and 6 tablespoons sugar. Serve immediately.

12 large prunes	Deep fat for frying
12 blanched almonds	1½ ounces semisweet chocolate
Batter for *Beignets à la Dijonnaise* (see Index)	6 tablespoons sugar
	YIELD: 3 to 4 servings

Hjortetak (Norwegian Doughnuts)

These Norwegian doughnuts are far too elegant for breakfast-coffee dunking. Serve them at the afternoon tea table.

Beat 2 eggs with ½ cup sugar until thick and light. Sift 2 scant cups flour with ¼ teaspoon cream of tartar and ½ teaspoon powdered cardamom. Add the dry ingredients alternately with 2 tablespoons brandy and ⅓ cup butter, melted. Mix the dough thoroughly, and chill for ½ hour in the freezer.

On a lightly floured board, roll out the dough ⅓ inch thick. With a doughnut cutter, cut out circles of dough, and deep fry at 370° until golden brown. Drain on absorbent paper, and dust copiously with confectioners' sugar.

2 eggs	2 tablespoons brandy
½ cup sugar	⅓ cup butter, melted
2 scant cups flour	Deep fat for frying
¼ teaspoon cream of tartar	Confectioners' sugar
½ teaspoon powdered cardamom	YIELD: about 24 doughnuts

Gretel's *Arme Ritter* (Rolled French Toast)

What we call French Toast is known as *Pain Perdu* (lost bread) in French, and *Arme Ritter* (poor knight) in German. Though the chefs had the same idea, whoever christens recipes assuredly did not. In Gretel's version, the basic idea is a French Toast, but much glorified.

Trim the crusts from 18 thin slices of white bread, and, with the palm of your hand or a rolling pin, flatten each slice. Spread each slice with 1 teaspoon butter, softened, then with 2 teaspoons of strawberry, raspberry or any well-flavored thick jam. Roll up each slice, and leave, cut side down, until ready to fry.

Make a batter: In a bowl, combine 2 lightly beaten eggs, 1 cup flour, 1 teaspoon baking powder, 1 tablespoon sugar, ½ cup milk, and 3 tablespoons brandy. (Preparation up to this point may be done in advance.)

Preheat oven to 250°. Have ready a baking sheet covered with several thicknesses of brown paper. Dip the bread rolls in batter, coating them liberally, and deep fry at 370° until golden brown on one side, then turn and fry until golden brown on the other side. Drain on absorbent paper for 1 minute, then transfer to the paper-covered baking sheet, and keep hot in the oven until all the rolls are fried. Dust generously with confectioners' sugar, and serve immediately.

If you wish, you may fry them in advance. A half hour before servingtime, preheat oven to 450°. Just before servingtime, place the fried *Arme Ritter* on the paper-covered baking sheet, and reheat for 5 minutes, or until very crisp and hot. They are just as good this way, if not better!

18 thin slices white bread	1 teaspoon baking powder
6 tablespoons butter	1 tablespoon sugar
¾ cup strawberry, raspberry, or any well-flavored thick jam	½ cup milk
	3 tablespoons brandy
2 eggs	Deep fat for frying
1 cup flour	Confectioners' sugar

YIELD: 9 servings

Bignè di Ricotta (Deep-Fried Cheese Puffs)

Serve these Italian puffs either as directed, or with Brandied Black Cherry Sauce (see Index), or Rum Sauce (see Index).

In a bowl, mix 3 lightly beaten eggs, 2 tablespoons sugar, and 1 pound *ricotta*. (If you cannot obtain *ricotta*, substitute 1 pound of cottage cheese, sieved.) Into the bowl, sift together: 1 cup flour, ¼ teaspoon salt, and 4 teaspoons baking powder. Mix well, and let the batter stand for 1 hour.

In a deep pot, heat oil or shortening to 370°. Drop the batter into the hot fat by tablespoonfuls, and deep fry for 3 minutes, or until golden brown. Drain on absorbent paper, dust very generously with confectioners' sugar, and serve immediately. (Or, as you fry them, place on a paper-covered baking sheet, and keep hot in a 250° oven until all the puffs are fried.)

3 eggs	¼ teaspoon salt
2 tablespoons sugar	4 teaspoons baking powder
1 pound *ricotta*	Deep fat for frying
1 cup flour	Confectioners' sugar

YIELD: 2 to 2½ dozen puffs

Crème Frite, Marianne (Fried Cream Croquettes)

Crème frite, fried cream, should be more widely known, and served more often than it generally is. In addition to being so very good, it requires practically no last-minute attention.

In a saucepan, mix 2 lightly beaten eggs, 3 tablespoons sugar, and 5 tablespoons of rice flour (or cornstarch). Gradually add 1½ cups milk, stir until smooth, and cook, over low heat, stirring constantly, until very thick. Remove from heat, add 1 tablespoon lemon juice, and pour into a greased 5-by-9-inch bread pan. Chill thoroughly.

Make a batter by beating together: 1 egg, ½ cup flour, ½ teaspoon baking powder, and ⅓ cup milk. Cut the chilled cream into 10 equal portions, dip each portion into the batter, and deep fry at 375° until gold. Drain on absorbent paper, and place, in a single layer, in a greased, shallow, ovenproof dish. (Preparation up to this point may be done in advance.)

Twenty-five minutes before servingtime, preheat oven to 450°. Sprinkle ⅓ cup sugar over the fried cream, and bake about 15 minutes, or until the sugar caramelizes.

2 eggs	1 egg
3 tablespoons sugar	½ cup flour
5 tablespoons rice flour or corn-starch	½ teaspoon baking powder
1½ cups milk	⅓ cup milk
1 tablespoon lemon juice	⅓ cup sugar

YIELD: 5 servings

Eva's *Zwetschkenknödel* (Plum Dumplings)

Plum-filled dumplings are a popular Middle European dessert of peasant origin. There are innumerable recipes for the dough, and the ingredients vary. I prefer this one with cheese; it seems to produce a lighter dumpling.

In a bowl, mix together ½ pound pot cheese, sieved, 2 eggs, 2 tablespoons of soft butter, ¼ teaspoon salt, and ¾ cup flour, until you have a smooth but sticky dough. Chill the dough in the freezer for 1 hour, or until it can be rolled. On a heavily-floured board, and with a well-floured rolling pin, roll out the dough to a large ⅛-inch-thick rectangle. (As you roll the dough keep loosening it from the board with a spatula, and dust the board with additional flour if necessary.)

Pit 30 medium-size blue plums, and fill each cavity with ½ teaspoon sugar. Cut the dough into 30 squares, each large enough to enclose a plum. With well-floured hands, wrap each plum in a square of dough, and seal the edges well. Simmer in a large pot of lightly salted water until the dumplings rise to the surface. (Cook a few at a time, watching that they don't stick to the bottom of the pot.) Remove the dumplings with a slotted spoon, and chill. (Preparation up to this point may be done in advance.)

Shortly before servingtime, melt 2 tablespoons butter in a large heavy frying pan. Sauté the dumplings until golden on all sides, adding more butter as necessary. Serve hot with a selection of several of these accompaniments: melted butter, sugar, cinnamon, chopped walnuts, cottage cheese, poppy seeds, sour cream.

½ pound pot cheese	Choice of 2 or 3 of the following:
2 eggs	Melted butter
2 tablespoons butter	Sugar
¼ teaspoon salt	Cinnamon
¾ cup flour	Chopped walnuts
30 medium-size blue plums	Cottage cheese
About ⅓ cup sugar	Poppy seeds
Butter for frying	Sour cream

YIELD: 30 dumplings

Cannoli (Filled Deep-Fried Pastries)

These Italian deep-fried pastries are utterly delectable, and they may be prepared in advance and stored in a tightly-sealed tin or in the freezer. Fill them with custard, whipped cream, ice cream, or the traditional (and I think the best) *ricotta* filling. To make them, you will need special metal tubes, 5½ inches long and ½ to 1 inch in diameter, that are available in well-stocked hardware shops or in the housewares section of a department store. They are also used to make Lady Locks pastries, and are identified by either name.

First make the *ricotta* filling, and chill for 2 hours before using. Sieve 1 pound *ricotta* (or cottage cheese) into a mixing bowl. Add ⅓ cup confectioners' sugar, 1 teaspoon vanilla, ½ ounce of dark sweet chocolate, coarsely grated, and 2 tablespoons each minced candied citron, candied cherries, and candied lemon peel. Mix together, and chill.

Into a small bowl, sift 1 cup flour, ⅛ teaspoon salt, and 2 tablespoons sugar. With a pastry blender, cut in 1 tablespoon butter until the mixture resembles meal. Beat 1 egg with ½ tablespoon each white vinegar and water, add to the flour, and mix until you have a smooth dough. Turn out onto a lightly floured board, divide into 12 pieces, and roll each piece to a circle large enough to fit around the *cannoli* tube with a ¾-inch overlap. Place circles of dough around lightly greased tubes, a few at a time. Moisten edge with cold water, press overlap securely, and deep fry at 375° until the *cannoli* are golden brown. Drain on absorbent paper, and remove tubes when they are cool enough to handle. Shortly before servingtime, fill with *ricotta* or other filling, and dust generously with confectioners' sugar.

1 pound *ricotta* (or cottage cheese)	1 cup flour
⅓ cup confectioners' sugar	⅛ teaspoon salt
1 teaspoon vanilla	2 tablespoons sugar
½ ounce dark sweet chocolate, coarsely grated	1 tablespoon butter
2 tablespoons minced candied citron	1 egg
	½ tablespoon white vinegar
2 tablespoons minced candied cherries	½ tablespoon water
	Fat for deep frying
2 tablespoons minced candied lemon peel	Confectioners' sugar

YIELD: about 12 *cannoli*

FRUITS

HOT FRUITS

Bananas *con Arroz* (Bananas with Rice)

Pommes Pralinées (Almond-Crusted Apples)

Baked Pears *Roosendaal*

Fruits Victoire (Flaming Meringued Fruit)

Pommes Madame (Macaroon Apple Dessert)

Baked Tutti Frutti

Ananász Kecskemét (Baked Filled Pineapple)

Pesche Ripiene di Mama Angela
(Angela's Stuffed Peaches)

Flaming Strawberries *à l'Orange*

Blueberries Helsinki

Bananas *con Arroz* (Bananas with Rice)

Peel 6 ripe bananas, slice in half lengthwise and crosswise, and marinate in ¼ cup sweet sherry for 45 minutes.

In the meantime, cook the milk rice: Into 2 cups of boiling water, pour ½ cup of long-grain rice, boil for 5 minutes, and drain. Add 2¼ cups milk, ¼ teaspoon salt, ⅓ cup Vanilla Sugar (see Index), and bring to a boil, stirring occasionally. Turn heat low, cover pot, and simmer for about 30 minutes, or until rice is tender and liquid almost absorbed. Remove from heat, and stir in 3 tablespoons of sweet sherry. Spread milk rice in a large, shallow, ovenproof dish, buttered. (If desired, the milk rice may be cooked ahead.)

Preheat broiler. Arrange bananas on rice. To the remaining marinade, add 6 tablespoons butter, melted, and ⅓ cup orange marmalade and spoon over bananas and rice. Place dish on broiler rack 3 inches from heat until edges of bananas begin to brown.

6 ripe bananas
¼ cup sweet sherry
2 cups boiling water
½ cup long-grain rice
2¼ cups milk
¼ teaspoon salt

⅓ cup Vanilla Sugar (see Index)
3 tablespoons sweet sherry
6 tablespoons butter
⅓ cup orange marmalade
YIELD: 8 servings

Pommes Pralinées (Almond-Crusted Apples)

Peel, core, and quarter 3 pounds of large cooking apples. Cook, covered, over low heat, with 2 tablespoons each lemon juice and water, and ¼ cup sugar, until soft. Remove 6 apple quarters, turn up heat, and cook remaining fruit, uncovered, until liquid evaporates. Mash fruit until puréed, and spread in a 1-inch-thick layer in a shallow baking dish. Arrange reserved apple quarters, rounded side up, on top of purée. In a small bowl, mix together 1 unbeaten egg white with ⅔ cup confectioners' sugar and 1 teaspoon cornstarch. Stir vigorously for 3 minutes, then add ⅓ cup chopped or slivered almonds. (Preparation up to this point may be done in advance.)

Thirty-five minutes before servingtime, preheat oven to 350°. Spread almond mixture on top of apples and purée, and bake for 25 minutes, or until top is crusty and gold.

3 pounds large cooking apples	⅔ cup confectioners' sugar
2 tablespoons lemon juice	1 teaspoon cornstarch
2 tablespoons water	⅓ cup chopped or slivered
¼ cup sugar	almonds
1 egg white	

YIELD: 6 servings

Baked Pears *Roosendaal*

Preheat oven to 300°. In a saucepan, over medium heat, cook 1 cup sugar, ½ cup water, and 1½ tablespoons lemon juice until the sugar is dissolved. Peel and core 6 large pears that are slightly underripe. Cut a thin slice from the blossom end so that the pears will stand upright. Place them, upright, in a baking dish just large enough to accommodate the fruit. Pour the syrup over the pears, and bake about 1½ hours, basting every 15 minutes, until the fruit is very tender and a mellow golden brown. Serve hot with a slice of ice-cold hard sauce, below. (You may bake the pears in advance, and reheat, covered, in the oven.)

Ginger Hard Sauce: Cream ¾ cup confectioners' sugar, ¼ cup sweet butter, and 1 tablespoon heavy cream until light and fluffy. Fold in 2 to 3 tablespoons candied ginger, finely minced. Chill until firm enough to shape into a roll 2 inches in diameter. At servingtime, cut into 6 slices, and serve 1 slice with each hot pear.

1 cup sugar	¼ cup sweet butter
½ cup water	1 tablespoon heavy cream
1½ tablespoons lemon juice	2 to 3 tablespoons candied
6 large pears	ginger, finely minced
¾ cup confectioners' sugar	

YIELD: 6 servings

Fruits Victoire (Flaming Meringued Fruit)

For this dish use any stewed fresh fruit (peeled and cored) or berries; or use any canned fruit.

Drain and reserve the juice of 6 pitted, stewed or canned peaches (or any other fruit), or 4 cups stewed or canned berries or pitted cherries. (Measure the berries or cherries after draining.) In a saucepan, over high heat, boil the juice until it is reduced to a heavy syrup. Divide the fruit or berries among 6 small baking dishes, and spoon a little of the syrup over each portion. (Or, put the fruit in a large shallow baking dish that can go to the table.)

Thirty to forty minutes before servingtime, beat 3 egg whites until they form moist peaks, gradually add ½ cup sugar, continuing to beat until thick and shiny. Spoon the meringue into a pastry tube fitted with a star-shaped opening, and pipe over the top of the fruit in a decorative spiral. Preheat oven to 325°. Fifteen minutes before servingtime, place in the oven for about 13 minutes, or until the meringue is flecked with color.

Warm ½ cup light rum and ignite. Pour the flaming rum over the fruit, and bring the blazing fruit to the table.

6 stewed or canned peaches, or 4 cups stewed or canned berries or cherries	3 egg whites
	½ cup sugar
	½ cup light rum

YIELD: 6 servings

Pommes Madame (Macaroon Apple Dessert)

Preheat oven to 400°. Mix 8 crumbled almond macaroons with ½ cup sugar. Peel and core 6 large cooking apples. Slice thinly, and arrange in layers in a buttered 1½- to 2-quart baking dish, sprinkling each layer with part of the macaroon-sugar mixture. Cover, and bake for 10 minutes. Uncover, and bake about 10 minutes longer, or until apples are tender.

Beat 3 eggs with ¼ cup sugar, then add 1 cup milk and ½ cup light cream. Pour mixture over apples, and bake 15 minutes longer, or until the custard is set and the top golden.

8 almond macaroons	¼ cup sugar
½ cup sugar	1 cup milk
6 large cooking apples	½ cup light cream
3 eggs	

YIELD: 6 servings

Baked Tutti Frutti

Preheat oven to 325°. Drain a 1-pound can each black or red cherries, apricots, red or green plums, and pineapple chunks. Remove any pits. On the bottom of a deep 1½- to 2-quart baking dish, spread the cherries in an even layer. Cover with ⅓ cup seeded raisins, ¼ cup chopped walnuts, 2 tablespoons brown sugar, and dot with 1 tablespoon butter. Cover with successive layers of the other fruits, separating each layer with an equal quantity of raisins, walnuts, brown sugar, and butter (except over the top layer). Pour ½ cup brandy over the fruit. Sprinkle ⅓ cup zwieback crumbs mixed with ½ cup brown sugar over the top, and dot with 2 tablespoons butter. Bake for 25 minutes, or until the top is gold. Serve hot.

1 1-pound can black or red cherries	1 cup seeded raisins
	¾ cup chopped walnuts
1 1-pound can apricots	6 tablespoons brown sugar
1 1-pound can red or green plums	3 tablespoons butter
	½ cup brandy
1 1-pound can pineapple chunks	⅓ cup zwieback crumbs
	½ cup brown sugar

YIELD: 10 to 12 servings

Ananász Kecskemét (Baked Filled Pineapple)

It is a good deal easier, I think, to master this recipe than to pronounce and spell its Hungarian name.

Preheat oven to 400°. Cut the top from a large ripe pineapple (preferably Hawaiian), and scoop out the fruit, being careful not to pierce the shell. Discard the hard center core, and dice the fruit. Toss the pineapple with 4 almond macaroons, crumbled, ¼ cup slivered dried apricots, and ¾ cup apricot jam. Pile the fruit into the shell, cover with a piece of foil, and place in a small baking dish. Bake for ½ hour, remove the foil, and bake ½ hour longer. Remove the pineapple to a serving platter. Heat ¼ cup light rum, ignite, and pour over the fruit. Bring to the table blazing.

1 large, ripe pineapple   ¾ cup apricot jam
4 almond macaroons   ¼ cup light rum
¼ cup slivered dried apricots

YIELD: 6 servings

Pesche Ripiene di Mama Angela
(Angela's Stuffed Peaches)

Preheat oven to 375°. Dip 12 large peaches in boiling water, and slip off the skins. Cut the fruit in half and discard the pits. In a small bowl, mix together: ½ cup finely chopped walnuts, ¼ cup each finely chopped pistachio nuts, sugar, and peach jam, and 2 tablespoons each minced candied cherries and citron. Fill the peach cavities with the mixture, and put the halves together. Roll the filled peaches in 3 tablespoons peach jam, then in ¾ cup finely chopped walnuts. Place the peaches in a shallow baking dish just large enough to accommodate them. Pour ¼ cup melted butter over the fruit, and bake for about 20 minutes, or until the fruit is tender. Serve the fruit warm.

12 large peaches   2 tablespoons minced candied
½ cup finely chopped walnuts   citron
¼ cup finely chopped pistachio   3 tablespoons peach jam
  nuts   ¾ cup finely chopped walnuts
¼ cup sugar   ¼ cup melted butter
¼ cup peach jam
2 tablespoons minced candied
  cherries

YIELD: 12 servings

Flaming Strawberries *à l'Orange*

Make this in a chafing dish at the table. The aroma is second only to the flavor! Flaming Strawberries are superb over ice cream, too. (When strawberries are not in season, substitute 16 well-drained canned peach or pear halves.)

Hull, wash, and drain 1½ quarts of large ripe strawberries. With a vegetable peeler or small sharp knife, peel the zest (thin orange skin without any of the underlying white pith) of a large juice orange. Squeeze and reserve the juice. Cut the zest into julienne, boil in a small quantity of water for 5 minutes, and drain.

In the blazer of a chafing dish, over direct heat, melt 2 tablespoons butter. Add ¼ cup sugar, and cook until the mixture turns pale gold. Add the zest of the orange, and cook, stirring constantly, for 1 minute. Add 2 tablespoons each cognac, kirsch, and Grand Marnier, and cook until bubbling. Add the strawberries, and heat, stirring gently to coat them with syrup. (Do not overcook, or the berries will start to draw juice.) Ignite the liquor, and when the flames die out, pour in the orange juice. Serve immediately.

If you do not have a chafing dish, use a decorative pan that can come to the table. Prepare the strawberries on the stove, and serve directly from the pan.

1½ quarts large, ripe strawberries	¼ cup sugar
1 large juice orange	2 tablespoons cognac
2 tablespoons butter	2 tablespoons kirsch
	2 tablespoons Grand Marnier

YIELD: 8 servings

Blueberries Helsinki

Preheat oven to 350°. Wash and drain 1 quart of blueberries.
Mix 3 tablespoons sugar, 1 tablespoon flour, and 2 teaspoons
grated orange rind. Sprinkle over the berries, toss gently, and
pour into a 1-quart baking dish. Beat 1 egg lightly and combine with 3 tablespoons sugar, 1 teaspoon grated orange rind, 6
almond macaroons, crumbled, and 2 tablespoons of vanilla
cooky crumbs. Spoon this mixture over the berries, and bake
for 25 minutes, or until a crust-like top forms. Serve warm.

1 quart blueberries	3 tablespoons sugar
3 tablespoons sugar	1 teaspoon grated orange rind
1 tablespoon flour	6 almond macaroons
2 teaspoons grated orange rind	2 tablespoons vanilla cooky
1 egg	crumbs

YIELD: 6 servings

COLD FRUITS

Raspberry *Kissel* (Raspberry Pudding)

Fragole Dama Bianca (Strawberries with Cream Meringue)

Pears *à la Crème* (Pears in a Cream)

Pears Lucienne (Baked Pear Dessert)

Capri (Berries with Whipped Cream and Wine Sauce)

Fresh Figs Valencia

Bananas Estoril

Poire à l'Étoile (Pears in a Caramelized Cream)

Mormors Persikor (Grandmother's Peaches)

161

Raspberry *Kissel* (Raspberry Pudding)

Other fruit or berries may be substituted for raspberries, and fresh fruit or berries may be used instead of frozen; 1 pint of fresh berries is the approximate equivalent of 2 frozen 10-ounce packages. Generally berries are puréed for *Kissel*, rather than left whole as this recipe indicates. I find the flavor superior and the texture more interesting with whole berries, or fruit cut into small pieces rather than mashed. If, however, their appearance is not prime, I do recommend that you purée them.

Defrost and drain four 10-ounce packages of frozen raspberries. Measure the juice, and add water, if necessary, to make 2 cups of liquid. In a saucepan, mix 3 tablespoons potato starch with a little of the juice, stir in remaining juice, and cook over low heat, stirring constantly, until juice becomes thick and clear. This happens immediately after it comes to a boil. Remove from heat and add berries. Pour into a serving bowl and sprinkle ½ teaspoon sugar over the surface to prevent the formation of a skin. Cool and chill.

Whip ½ cup heavy cream with 1 tablespoon sugar until somewhat thickened but not stiff. Pour into a sauceboat and pass separately with the *Kissel*.

To make *Kissel* from fresh raspberries, stem, wash, and drain 1 quart of raspberries. Mash a scant half of the berries through a sieve, or purée in an electric blender. Measure the purée, and add water, if necessary, to make 2 cups. Dissolve 4 teaspoons potato starch in 2 tablespoons cold water (you need less starch for the purée than for the juice of frozen berries), and pour into a saucepan. Add purée, ½ teaspoon lemon juice, and ⅓ cup sugar, or more, to taste. Cook, chill, and serve as for *Kissel* of frozen raspberries.

162

Kissel of frozen raspberries	*Kissel* of fresh raspberries
4 10-ounce packages frozen raspberries	1 quart raspberries
3 tablespoons potato starch	4 teaspoons potato starch
½ teaspoon sugar	2 tablespoons cold water
½ cup heavy cream	½ teaspoon lemon juice
1 tablespoon sugar	⅓ cup sugar
	YIELD: 6 servings

Fragole Dama Bianca
(Strawberries with Cream Meringue)

Four hours ahead, stem, wash, and drain 1 quart of firm, ripe strawberries. In a bowl, mix ¼ cup almond paste with ⅓ cup orange juice and 2 tablespoons sugar. Slice berries into the bowl, mix gently with almond paste mixture, and refrigerate.

Two hours before servingtime (no earlier or the meringue cream won't hold up), beat 2 egg whites until foamy, gradually add 6 tablespoons sugar, and continue to beat until meringue is thick and glossy. Fold in ½ cup heavy cream, beaten stiff, and ¼ cup sour cream. Pour berries into serving bowl, spoon cream mixture on top, and refrigerate.

Try this recipe, too, with peaches or raspberries or both.

1 quart strawberries	2 egg whites
¼ cup almond paste	6 tablespoons sugar
⅓ cup orange juice	½ cup heavy cream
2 tablespoons sugar	¼ cup sour cream
	YIELD: 8 servings

Pears *à la Crème* (Pears in a Cream)

Peel and core (leave the stems on) 8 large firm pears. Cut a thin slice from the bottom of each, so that pears will stand upright. In a pan large enough to accommodate pears in a single layer, dissolve ½ cup sugar in 1 cup water and the juice of ½ lemon. Add pears, cover pot, and simmer fruit about 30 to 45 minutes, or until tender. Remove fruit, drain, and cool.

In another saucepan, combine 2 tablespoons cornstarch, 5 tablespoons sugar, ⅟₁₆ teaspoon salt, 2 eggs, and 2 cups milk. Over low heat, stirring constantly, cook for about 10 minutes, or until custard thickens. Remove from heat, add ½ teaspoon vanilla, and cool.

Two hours before servingtime, simmer 2 cups water in a shallow pan. At the same time, in a small pot, over high heat, cook ⅔ cup sugar, 3 tablespoons water, and ½ cup blanched almonds, chopped, until the mixture turns a pale caramel color. Place the pot of caramel in the pan of simmering water. Working very quickly, apply some of the nut caramel to the top portion of each pear. (The pan of simmering water helps to keep the caramel liquid enough to work with. If it becomes too stiff and granular before you are finished, add 1 teaspoon water, and liquefy over low heat. A caramel must always be taken from the heat as it begins to turn color; it continues to cook and darken for a minute or so after it is removed from the heat.)

Assemble the dessert just before servingtime; otherwise the juice contained in the pears will dilute the custard sauce. Pour the custard into a shallow serving bowl, stand the pears upright in the sauce, and serve.

8 large firm pears	2 eggs
½ cup sugar	2 cups milk
1 cup water	½ teaspoon vanilla
Juice of ½ lemon	⅔ cup sugar
2 tablespoons cornstarch	3 tablespoons water
5 tablespoons sugar	½ cup blanched almonds,
⅟₁₆ teaspoon salt	chopped

YIELD: 8 servings

Pears Lucienne (Baked Pear Dessert)

Peel, core, and slice 4 pounds of firm ripe pears (about 7 large pears). In a large saucepan, place pears and 3¼ cups sugar in alternating layers. Add 3 tablespoons lemon juice, cover pot, and cook over very low heat for 3 hours until juices are syrupy and the pears a deep wine color. Remove from heat, purée in a food mill, or press through a sieve. Stir in ¼ pound plus 1 tablespoon butter and 1 teaspoon vanilla, and pour into a lightly oiled 1-quart mold. Refrigerate for 6 hours or overnight. Unmold on serving platter, and serve with a pitcher of sweet or sour cream passed separately.

4 pounds firm ripe pears	1 teaspoon vanilla
3¼ cups sugar	Sweet or sour cream
3 tablespoons lemon juice	
¼ pound plus 1 tablespoon butter	

YIELD: 8 servings

Capri
(Berries with Whipped Cream and Wine Sauce)

Hull, wash, and drain 1 pint of raspberries and 1 pint of strawberries, and pour into a bowl. Mix ¼ cup sugar with ¼ cup Marsala wine, and pour over berries. Chill for 2 hours, tossing berries occasionally. Whip 1½ cups heavy cream until very stiff with 6 tablespoons sugar, and chill. (To whip cream very stiff, chill the cream, bowl, and beater for at least 1 hour before whipping.)

At servingtime, make 1 recipe Wine *Chaudeau* (see Index). Spoon whipped cream into the bottom of dessert dishes, drain berries, and place on top of cream. Pass warm Wine *Chaudeau* separately.

1 pint raspberries	1½ cups heavy cream
1 pint strawberries	6 tablespoons sugar
¼ cup sugar	1 recipe Wine *Chaudeau* (see
¼ cup Marsala wine	Index)

YIELD: 8 servings

Fresh Figs Valencia

Mix ¼ pound cream cheese with ¼ cup bitter orange marmalade. Make an incision in the bottom of 24 large fresh figs (if possible, choose 12 green figs, and 12 black), and fill with the cheese mixture. Peel and remove all the white pith from 6 large eating oranges. Cut off and discard the top and bottom slices, and cut the remainder into 24 even slices. Discard pits.

Arrange a bed of leaves on a serving platter (grape leaves, if you can get them), pile the figs in a pyramid in the center (alternating green and black fruit), and ring with overlapping orange slices. Mix 1½ cups sour cream with ½ cup bitter orange marmalade, and pass this sauce separately in a sauceboat.

¼ pound cream cheese	Decorative leaves
¼ cup bitter orange marmalade	1½ cups sour cream
24 large fresh figs	½ cup bitter orange marmalade
6 large eating oranges	

YIELD: 12 servings

Bananas Estoril

In the bottom of a deep crystal serving bowl, place a layer of 6 ripe bananas, thinly sliced. With a fork, crush 1 quart of raspberries, add sugar to taste, and spread over the bananas. Whip 1 cup heavy cream until stiff with 4 tablespoons sugar, and spoon the cream over the berries. Over the cream sprinkle 4 almond macaroons, crumbled, and ¼ cup candied fruits, very finely minced. Chill for 1 hour before serving.

6 ripe bananas	4 tablespoons sugar
1 quart of raspberries	4 almond macaroons
Sugar	¼ cup candied fruits, very finely
1 cup heavy cream	minced

YIELD: 6 servings

Poires à l'Étoile (Pears in a Caramelized Cream)

L'Étoile is one of the newer Parisian restaurants, and, I think, one of the best, old or new. I have made this dessert with strawberries too; either way, it's superb.

In a saucepan, dissolve ½ cup sugar in ¾ cup water. Peel, core, and quarter 6 firm pears, and poach them in the syrup until tender. Drain, and cool. (If you use strawberries, hull, wash, and drain 3 cups of berries, but do not cook them.)

In another saucepan, mix 4 egg yolks, 4 teaspoons flour, ⅛ teaspoon salt, and ⅓ cup Vanilla Sugar (see Index). Gradually add 1⅓ cups hot milk, and cook over low heat, stirring constantly, until the custard is thick. Do not allow to boil. Cool completely, fold in ¾ cup heavy cream whipped until stiff, and chill thoroughly. Place the cooled pears (or berries) in a deep 8-inch baking dish (a *soufflé* dish is fine), and pour the chilled custard over the fruit.

Heat a salamander over medium heat for 10 minutes, or until red-hot, sprinkle ½ cup sugar over the surface of the cream, and pass the salamander quickly over the sugar to caramelize it. Lacking a salamander, put ½ cup sugar in a small heavy saucepan over medium heat, and heat, stirring occasionally, until the sugar dissolves and turns caramel color. Working quickly, before the caramel stiffens, dribble it, by spoonfuls, over the surface of the chilled custard. (This is why you chill the custard thoroughly; the caramel sets in a brittle glaze on contact with the ice-cold cream.)

Replace in the refrigerator until servingtime. When you serve the pears, tap the glaze with a spoon to shatter it. For this reason, it is preferable to serve *Poires à l'Étoile* at the table. Show off your handiwork, before you shatter the effect!

½ cup sugar
¾ cup water
6 firm pears (or 3 cups strawberries)
4 egg yolks
4 teaspoons flour

⅛ teaspoon salt
⅓ cup Vanilla Sugar (see Index)
1⅓ cups hot milk
¾ cup heavy cream
½ cup sugar

YIELD: 6 to 8 servings

Mormor's Persikor (Grandmother's Peaches)

I have never known this recipe by any name other than its literal translation from Swedish, Grandmother's Peaches.

Dip 6 medium-size peaches into boiling water, and slip off the skins. In a saucepan, bring 1 cup light brown sugar and 1 cup water to a boil. Slice the peaches, and simmer in the syrup until just tender. Cool the fruit, and chill it.

Just before servingtime, drain the peaches. Mix 2 tablespoons light brown sugar, ¼ teaspoon powdered cardamom, and ¼ cup sour cream. Add 1 cup of slightly softened vanilla ice cream, fold in the sliced peaches, and spoon into a serving bowl. Sprinkle ¼ cup toasted slivered almonds on the top, and serve immediately.

6 medium-size peaches	¼ cup sour cream
1 cup light brown sugar	1 cup vanilla ice cream
1 cup water	¼ cup toasted slivered almonds
2 tablespoons light brown sugar	
¼ teaspoon powdered carda-mom	

YIELD: 6 servings

PUDDINGS

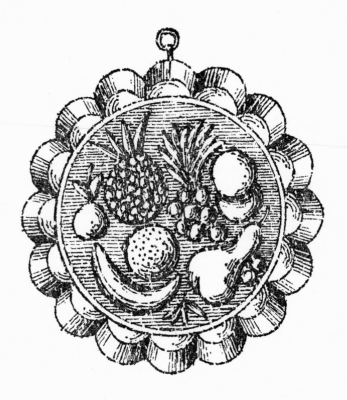

HOT PUDDINGS

Killarney Steamed Pudding

Whitchurch Pudding

Wine *Chaudeau*

Madame Bonné's Steamed Pudding

Gräfin Ilse's Pudding

Koffiepudding (Coffee Pudding)

Nudelpudding mit Aprikosen (Apricot Noodle Pudding)

Salzburger Nockerl (Salzburg *Soufflé* Pudding)

Matzoth Pudding

Killarney Steamed Pudding

Don't be put off by the seemingly homely ingredients of this pudding, and banish it from company menus. Though it is a hearty dessert, best after a light meal, it has a delicate flavor and a wonderful texture that none will associate with breakfast fare. Irish or Scotch oatmeal is preferable; substitute the domestic if you must, but then you will need 1⅓ cups oatmeal. Reduce cooking time in the double boiler to 40 minutes.

In the top of a double boiler, covered, over medium heat, cook together 9 tablespoons of Irish oatmeal and 3 cups of milk, for 1½ hours. To the cooked oatmeal, add 6 tablespoons Irish honey, 3 tablespoons butter, melted, ¾ cup light raisins, 1 teaspoon cinnamon, ½ teaspoon salt, ⅓ cup ground almonds, and 3 egg yolks. Mix well, fold in 3 egg whites, beaten stiff, and pour into a well-buttered 1½-quart pudding mold, fitted with a lid. (Lacking such a mold, use a shortening can with tight-fitting cover, or pour into a baking dish, cover top with foil, and tie securely.) Place in a pot, and fill pot to a depth of 2 inches with hot water. Cover pot and cook over medium heat for 1½ hours. Leave in mold for 5 minutes before turning out onto a serving platter. Serve with additional honey passed separately.

9 tablespoons Irish oatmeal	½ teaspoon salt
3 cups milk	⅓ cup ground almonds
6 tablespoons Irish honey	3 egg yolks
3 tablespoons butter	3 egg whites
¾ cup light raisins	Irish honey
1 teaspoon cinnamon	

YIELD: 6 to 8 servings

Whitchurch Pudding

In a saucepan, over low heat, cook 6 tablespoons of sugar until the sugar dissolves, and begins to take on a medium caramel color. Remove from heat for 2 minutes. Heat 1 cup of milk. Turn heat to medium, replace pan of caramelized sugar, and very gradually add the milk, stirring constantly. (Don't be alarmed; some of the sugar will harden.) Cook until the sugar melts again, stirring all the while. Remove from heat and cool while preparing remaining ingredients.

Mix ¾ cup ground hazelnuts with 1 tablespoon flour. Separate 6 eggs, and beat the whites stiff. To the sugar-milk mixture, add the nuts and flour, 1 teaspoon vanilla, 6 egg yolks, and ¼ cup very soft butter. Beat until smooth. Fold in the stiffly beaten whites, and pour into a well-buttered and sugared 1½-quart pudding mold, fitted with a lid. (Lacking such a mold, use a shortening can, or pour into a baking dish, cover top with foil, and tie securely.)

Cover mold, place in a pot, and fill pot to a depth of 2 inches with hot water. Cover pot and steam over medium heat for 55 minutes. Turn out onto a serving platter, and serve with a pitcher of heavy cream passed separately.

Like almost all steamed puddings, Whitchurch Pudding may be made in advance, or even frozen, and reheated. Butter the mold in which it was originally steamed, replace the pudding, cover, and steam according to directions above, until heated through.

6 tablespoons sugar	6 eggs
1 cup milk	1 teaspoon vanilla
¾ cup ground hazelnuts	¼ cup butter
1 tablespoon flour	Heavy cream

YIELD: 6 servings

Wine *Chaudeau*

Also known as *Zabaglione* in Italy, *Sabayon* in France.

In a heavy saucepan, place 4 egg yolks, ⅓ cup confectioners' sugar, ½ cup white wine, and ½ cup Marsala wine. With a wire whisk, over very low heat, beat rapidly, until the mixture is thick and light. Do not allow to boil. Remove from heat and pour into stemmed glasses or sherbets. Serve either warm or chilled. Slices of plain cake or slightly sweetened biscuits make a nice accompaniment.

If you serve Wine *Chaudeau* warm, make it at servingtime. To serve it chilled, make it no more than an hour in advance; otherwise it develops an unpleasant sticky surface.

Wine *Chaudeau* is also used as a sauce over fruit, pudding, or plain cake.

4 egg yolks	½ cup white wine
⅓ cup confectioners' sugar	½ cup Marsala wine

YIELD: 4 servings as dessert or 8 servings as sauce

Madame Bonné's Steamed Pudding

Sprinkle 4 almond macaroons, crumbled, with 2 tablespoons light rum. Plump ¼ cup light raisins in boiling water to cover. In a saucepan, using a whisk, beat 6 egg yolks with 6 tablespoons Vanilla Sugar (see Index), 2 tablespoons cornstarch, and ¼ teaspoon salt, until well blended. Gradually add 1 cup milk. Cook over low heat, stirring constantly, until custard is very thick (the consistency of a heavy cream sauce). Do not permit to boil. Remove from heat and cool for 10 minutes.

Meanwhile, butter the sides and bottom of a 2-quart pudding mold or shortening can with tight-fitting lid, and dust with 3 tablespoons fine dry bread crumbs. Drain raisins, and fold into custard. Break 6 ladyfingers into 5 or 6 pieces each. Beat 6 egg whites until stiff but not dry, and fold into custard. Pour batter into prepared mold, to a depth of 1 inch. Scatter half the ladyfingers over the batter, pour in another layer of batter, and scatter the macaroons over it. Cover with a third layer of batter, scatter with remaining ladyfingers, and finish with remaining batter. Cover mold, set in a large pot, fill to a depth of 2 inches with boiling water, cover pot and simmer for 1¾ hours. Turn out onto a serving platter, and serve with rum-flavored whipped cream or Vanilla Sauce (see Index) passed separately.

This pudding may be made in advance and reheated (see Whitchurch Pudding).

4 almond macaroons	1 cup milk
2 tablespoons light rum	Butter
¼ cup light raisins	3 tablespoons fine dry bread
6 egg yolks	crumbs
6 tablespoons Vanilla Sugar	6 ladyfingers
(see Index)	6 egg whites
2 tablespoons cornstarch	Rum-flavored whipped cream or
¼ teaspoon salt	Vanilla Sauce (see Index)

YIELD: 6 servings

Gräfin Ilse's Pudding

In the top of a double boiler, over boiling water, melt 3 ounces of semisweet chocolate. Cream ¼ pound plus 2 tablespoons sweet butter with ⅔ cup sugar until light and fluffy. Add 5 egg yolks, 1 tablespoon rum, and the melted chocolate. Beat well. Fold in ⅔ cup each ground almonds and hazelnuts, 3 tablespoons fine dry bread crumbs, and ½ cup raisins. Beat 5 egg whites until stiff but not dry, and fold into the chocolate mixture.

Butter a large pudding or melon mold with a tight-fitting cover, and dust with sugar. Pour the batter into the mold, filling it no more than two-thirds full (the pudding will rise), cover the mold, and place in a pot of simmering water that reaches two-thirds up the sides of the mold. Cover the pot, and steam for about 1¼ hours, or until the pudding is set. Let the pudding stand for 5 minutes, then turn out onto a serving platter. Serve immediately, with Chocolate Sauce #1 (see Index) passed separately. (You may keep the pudding hot for a while by turning off the heat and leaving it in the mold in hot water.)

3 ounces semisweet chocolate	⅔ cup ground hazelnuts
¼ pound plus 2 tablespoons sweet butter	3 tablespoons fine dry bread crumbs
⅔ cup sugar	½ cup raisins
5 egg yolks	5 egg whites
1 tablespoon rum	Chocolate Sauce #1 (see Index)
⅔ cup ground almonds	

YIELD: 8 servings

Koffiepudding (Coffee Pudding)

In a saucepan, over medium heat, melt ¼ pound less 1 tablespoon butter. Add ¾ cup plus 2 tablespoons flour, and stir until smooth. Gradually add ½ cup each hot milk and hot coffee, and 2 teaspoons instant coffee. Cook, stirring rapidly, until the mixture is smooth and leaves the sides of the pan. Remove from heat, and cool to lukewarm. Beat 5 egg yolks with ½ cup sugar until thick and light, and stir into cooled coffee mixture.

Beat 5 egg whites until stiff but not dry, and fold into mixture.

Butter a large pudding or melon mold with a tight-fitting cover, and dust with sugar. Pour the batter into the mold, filling it no more than two-thirds full (the pudding will rise), cover the mold, and place in a pot of simmering water that reaches two-thirds up the sides of the mold. Cover the pot, and steam for 50 to 60 minutes, or until the pudding is set. Let the pudding stand for 5 minutes, then turn out onto a serving platter, and serve immediately with a double recipe of Rum Sauce (see Index) passed separately.

¼ pound less 1 tablespoon butter	5 egg yolks
¾ cup plus 2 tablespoons flour	½ cup sugar
½ cup hot milk	5 egg whites
½ cup hot coffee	Double recipe Rum Sauce (see Index)
2 teaspoons instant coffee	YIELD: 8 servings

Nudelpudding mit Aprikosen
(Apricot Noodle Pudding)

Soak 1 pound of dried apricots in hot water to cover. Boil ½ pound of fine noodles according to package directions, and drain. Into the noodles, stir ¼ pound of butter, melted. Preheat oven to 350°. Cream 1 cup sugar, 3 ounces of cream cheese, the juice of 1 lemon, and 6 egg yolks until light and fluffy. Add the yolk mixture to the noodles. Beat 6 egg whites until stiff but not dry, and fold into the noodles.

Sprinkle ½ cup graham cracker crumbs over the bottom of a well-buttered shallow baking dish. Spoon half the noodle mixture over the crumbs. Drain the apricots, and place ¾ of them on the noodle layer. Spoon the remaining noodle mixture over the apricots, and place the remaining apricots, evenly spaced, on top. Bake for 1 hour.

1 pound dried apricots
½ pound fine noodles
¼ pound butter, melted
1 cup sugar
3 ounces cream cheese

Juice of 1 lemon
6 egg yolks
6 egg whites
½ cup graham cracker crumbs

YIELD: 8 to 10 servings

Salzburger Nockerl (Salzburg *Soufflé* Pudding)

This might be called a pudding; it could also be called a *soufflé*. A regional specialty of Salzburg, it is light and delicate in texture and taste. The recipes for it are legion; this is one of the best.

Preheat oven to 450°. Pour hot milk to a depth of ⅓ inch into a shallow 9- to 10-inch baking dish. Add 1 tablespoon of butter, cut into small pieces. Separate 6 eggs and reserve 5 egg yolks. Beat the 6 egg whites until stiff. Gradually add ⅔ cup Vanilla Sugar (see Index), continuing to beat until thick and shiny. Beat the 5 egg yolks with 2 tablespoons of sifted flour until well blended, and fold into the meringue. Spoon into baking dish. Place in the oven, reduce heat to 300°, and bake for 15 minutes.

With a large serving spoon, place portions of *Nockerl* on individual plates, and dust copiously with confectioners' sugar. Serve immediately.

Hot milk
1 tablespoon butter
6 egg whites
⅔ cup Vanilla Sugar (see
   Index)

5 egg yolks
2 tablespoons sifted flour
Confectioners' sugar

YIELD: 4 servings

Matzoth Pudding

Preheat oven to 375°. In a large bowl, soak 9 matzoths in boiling water to cover for 5 minutes. Drain the matzoths into a colander, and press out all excess moisture. Beat together 6 egg yolks, ½ cup brown sugar, 2 tablespoons butter, melted, ½ teaspoon each salt and cinnamon, and the grated rind of 1 orange. Stir in ¼ cup raisins, and 2 medium-size apples, peeled and coarsely grated. Add the matzoths, and fold in 6 stiffly beaten egg whites. Butter a shallow baking dish that can come to the table. Spoon in the mixture and bake for 40 minutes. Serve with a choice of jam, sour cream, or cinnamon and sugar.

9 matzoths	Grated rind of 1 orange
Boiling water	¼ cup raisins
6 egg yolks	2 medium-size apples
½ cup brown sugar	6 egg whites
2 tablespoons butter, melted	Jam, sour cream, and cinnamon
½ teaspoon salt	and sugar
½ teaspoon cinnamon	

YIELD: 6 to 8 servings

COLD PUDDINGS

Pashka (Russian Easter Dessert)

Oranges *Cernobbio*

Gubbasnus (Swedish Icebox Pudding)

Strawberry *Trollkräm* (Chiffon Pudding)

Raisin Bread and Butter Pudding

Mohrenkopf (Molded Cream with Chocolate Frosting)

Trifle (see English Dame Pettycock's Trifle Cake p. 7)

Pudim Lisboa (Brandied Pineapple-Cottage Cheese Mold)

Tsarina Rice

Pashka (Russian Easter Dessert)

This is a traditional, handsome, and delicious dessert that couldn't be simpler to prepare. In Russia at Eastertime, it was served with a yeast cake, *Kulich* (see Index), and the two make an excellent combination. Or, you may also serve *Pashka* this way: Unmold it on a crystal platter, surround it with mammoth, unhulled strawberries, and pass sour cream separately.

Place a double thickness of cheesecloth 18 inches square over the top of a mixing bowl. Allow the cloth to hang into the bowl to within 2 inches of the bottom. Tie, with string, around the outside of the bowl to hold the cloth securely in place.

Sieve 2 pounds of cottage cheese twice, or purée through a food mill. With a wooden spoon, in a large bowl, mix the cheese with ¼ pound softened butter, ½ cup sour cream, and ¾ cup Vanilla Sugar (see Index). Fold in ½ cup each slivered blanched almonds, and minced candied fruits, and 3 tablespoons chopped pistachio nuts. Pour into the cheesecloth, cover the cheese mixture with the overhanging pieces of cloth, place a weight on top (a can will do), and refrigerate for 6 hours, or overnight. Turn out onto a platter, and, with your hands and a spatula, shape into a high pyramid. Decorate with candied fruit peel, or surround with strawberries, and serve with sour cream.

2 pounds cottage cheese
¼ pound butter
½ cup sour cream
¾ cup Vanilla Sugar (see Index)
½ cup slivered blanched almonds

½ cup minced candied fruits
3 tablespoons chopped pistachio nuts
Candied fruit peel or large strawberries and sour cream
YIELD: serves 8

182

Oranges *Cernobbio*

Pour boiling water to cover over ¼ cup light raisins. Slice 3 oranges in half, crosswise, remove segments of fruit, and place them in a colander to drain. Scrape out all the white pith from the skins, and, with a small sharp knife or pinking shears, make a sawtooth edge around the top.

Sieve 3 cups of *ricotta* or cottage cheese twice, or pass through a food mill. To the cheese, add 4 egg yolks, ½ cup ground almonds, ⅓ cup sugar, ¼ cup minced candied orange peel, and 1 teaspoon almond extract. Drain the raisins thoroughly, add to the cheese, and stir the mixture gently. Spoon into the orange shells, and chill 2 hours, or longer. Shortly before servingtime, garnish with the drained orange segments.

¼ cup light raisins	⅓ cup sugar
3 oranges	¼ cup minced candied orange
3 cups *ricotta* or cottage cheese	peel
4 egg yolks	1 teaspoon almond extract
½ cup ground almonds	

YIELD: 6 servings

Gubbasnus (Swedish Icebox Pudding)

Gubbasnus means "old man's snuff." Why such a delectable dessert has been given such a name is a complete mystery to me. I have tried to find out; no one seems to know.

In a saucepan, place 2 medium-size apples, peeled, cored, and cut into eighths. Add ⅓ cup water, cover, and cook over low heat until apples are tender. Add more water only if necessary. Remove fruit, mash with a fork, and cool.

Trim crusts from heavy dark pumpernickel bread, and crumble enough to measure 1⅓ cups of very fine crumbs. (You will need about 6 slices.) Grate 2 ounces of dark sweet chocolate, and mix with the bread crumbs. Whip 1 cup heavy cream until stiff with 1 tablespoon sugar.

Cover the bottom of a 1-quart serving bowl with ⅓ of the bread crumbs and chocolate, spoon the applesauce over that, and cover with ⅓ of the cream. Next, spread ⅓ of the bread crumbs and chocolate over the cream. Cover with ⅔ cup softened currant jelly and then with ⅓ of the cream. Sprinkle with remaining bread crumbs and chocolate. Place the rest of the cream in a pastry tube, and press out in a decorative pattern over the top of the pudding. Chill for 4 hours.

2 medium-size apples	2 ounces dark sweet chocolate
⅓ cup water	1 cup heavy cream
1⅓ cups bread crumbs (heavy dark pumpernickel bread)	1 tablespoon sugar
	⅔ cup currant jelly

YIELD: 6 servings

Strawberry *Trollkräm* (Chiffon Pudding)

When you see the amount you start with, and watch it grow as it is whipped, you will agree with the Danes that trolls or magicians must have something to do with it.

In addition to serving the basic recipe as it stands, there are variations: Slice Spongecake Natasha (see Index) into 4 layers, or slice two 9-inch layers in half, crosswise, and spread *Trollkräm* between layers and on top and sides of cake, or prepare *Trollkräm*, spoon into 12 dessert dishes, top each serving with a Meringue (see Index), and ring with strawberries.

In the large bowl of the electric mixer, beat 1 egg white until foamy. Gradually add ¾ cup plus 2 tablespoons sugar, and continue to beat, at high speed, for 5 minutes. Add 1 cup mashed strawberries, and beat for 8 to 10 minutes longer, until the mixture is of a thick marshmallow-like texture. Turn into serving bowl, and chill until servingtime.

Trollkräm must be served the day it is made.

1 egg white	1 cup mashed strawberries
¾ cup plus 2 tablespoons sugar	YIELD: 8 servings

Raisin Bread and Butter Pudding

This appetizing dish is from the Hotel Connaught in London, where fine food is impeccably served in an atmosphere of restrained British elegance.

Preheat oven to 350°. Spread 2 tablespoons butter on 5 slices of firm raisin bread, cut the slices into ⅓-inch squares, and place in a deep 1½-quart baking dish. Scatter 3 tablespoons each light raisins and currants over the bread. Mix 5 lightly beaten eggs with ½ cup sugar, stir in 1 quart warm milk and 1 teaspoon vanilla, and strain into the baking dish. Set the dish in a large pan, fill the pan with hot water to a depth of 1 inch, and bake for 40 minutes, or until a silver knife blade inserted 1 inch from the edge of the pudding, comes out clean. Serve the pudding at room temperature.

2 tablespoons butter	5 eggs
5 slices of firm raisin bread	½ cup sugar
3 tablespoons light raisins	1 quart milk
3 tablespoons currants	1 teaspoon vanilla

YIELD: 6 to 8 servings

Mohrenkopf
(Molded Cream with Chocolate Frosting)

This Middle European dessert has always been, and, I am sure, will continue to be on my preferred list for elegant dinner parties. Never does it fail to evoke ecstatic appreciation and subsequent requests for the recipe, and this, as you know, is the ultimate compliment. Though you can make it 5 or 6 hours ahead of time, you may also prepare it a day ahead.

Soak 1 tablespoon gelatine in ½ cup cold water. Dissolve over low heat, and cool. Cream 6 tablespoons sweet butter with ½ cup sugar until light and fluffy. Beat in 3 egg yolks, one at a time, add 2 tablespoons cognac, 1 teaspoon vanilla, and the cooled gelatine. Stir well, and refrigerate for a few minutes until the mixture starts to thicken. Beat 1½ cups heavy cream until stiff, fold into gelatine mixture, and pour into a 5- to 6-cup bowl or melon mold that has been rinsed with cold water. Chill for 4 hours, or until firm. Run the tip of a small sharp knife around the inside of the mold to loosen cream. Dip mold into a pan of hot water for a few seconds. Invert mold, and turn out cream onto a serving platter.

Prepare ½ recipe Chocolate Frosting #3 (see Index). Spoon a little of the frosting on top of the cream, and, with the back of the spoon, tease the frosting over the cream. (I use a metal cereal or dessert spoon. Apply the frosting very lightly to a small area at a time. Don't worry if some of the frosting slides down onto the platter. This is inevitable, but you will rectify it later.) Chill for 1 hour, or until frosting is firm. Dip the tip of a sharp knife into cold water, trim bottom edges, and remove excess frosting from platter. With a moistened paper napkin, wipe the platter clean all around the mold. Shortly

before servingtime, whip ⅓ cup heavy cream until stiff, spoon
into a pastry tube fitted with a star tube, and pipe out little
rosettes of cream all around the base of the mold. Insert a
candied violet or lilac into each rosette.

1 tablespoon gelatine	1 teaspoon vanilla
½ cup cold water	1½ cups heavy cream
6 tablespoons sweet butter	½ recipe Chocolate Frosting #3
½ cup sugar	(see Index)
3 egg yolks	⅓ cup heavy cream
2 tablespoons cognac	Candied violets or lilacs

YIELD: 8 servings

Pudim Lisboa
(Brandied Pineapple-Cottage Cheese Mold)

In a saucepan, over low heat, simmer 2 cups of chopped ripe
pineapple with ⅓ cup sugar and ¼ cup water for 5 minutes.
Drain, and reserve both the fruit and the juice. (You may substitute canned crushed pineapple.) Measure the juice, and add
enough orange juice to make 2 cups of liquid. Soak 2 tablespoons gelatine in the fruit juice.

In another saucepan, mix 2 egg yolks, ½ cup each light
brown and granulated sugar, 2 tablespoons lemon juice, and
the grated rind of 1 orange. Add the gelatine mixture, and
cook, over low heat, until the sugars are dissolved. Remove
from heat, add 1 pound cottage cheese, sieved, 2 tablespoons
Portuguese brandy (or other brandy), and the reserved pineapple. Chill until thick, fold in 2 egg whites beaten until stiff
but not dry, and ½ cup heavy cream whipped until stiff.

Rinse a 2-quart mold or bowl with cold water, pour in the
pineapple cream, and chill until set. Run the tip of a sharp
knife around the inside of the mold to loosen the cream. Dip

the mold into hot water for a few seconds, and turn out the cream onto a serving platter.

Whip 1 cup heavy cream until stiff with ¼ cup sugar. Fold in the grated rind of 1 orange, and 2 tablespoons Portuguese brandy (or other brandy). Pass this sauce separately.

2 cups chopped ripe pineapple	1 pound cottage cheese
⅓ cup sugar	2 tablespoons Portuguese
¼ cup water	brandy (or other brandy)
Orange juice	2 egg whites
2 tablespoons gelatine	½ cup heavy cream
2 egg yolks	1 cup heavy cream
½ cup light brown sugar	¼ cup sugar
½ cup granulated sugar	Grated rind of 1 orange
2 tablespoons lemon juice	2 tablespoons Portuguese
Grated rind of 1 orange	brandy (or other brandy)

YIELD: 12 servings

Tsarina Rice

In the top of a double boiler, covered, cook ¼ cup unwashed rice with ¾ cup sugar in 3 cups milk for 1½ hours, or until rice is very tender. Fifteen minutes before the rice is done, soak 2 tablespoons gelatine in ¾ cup cold water. Add the soaked gelatine to the cooked rice, and stir until the gelatine is dissolved. Add ¼ teaspoon mace, ¼ teaspoon salt, and 1½ teaspoons each vanilla, almond extract, and rosewater (available at drugstores). Mix well, and chill.

When the mixture starts to set, fold in 1 cup heavy cream whipped until stiff, and 2 stiffly beaten egg whites. Rinse a 2-quart mold with cold water, pour in the rice mixture, and chill for several hours until set. Run the tip of a sharp knife around the inside of the mold to loosen the cream, dip the mold into hot water for a few seconds, and unmold onto a serving platter. Replace in the refrigerator until servingtime. Serve with Brandied Black Cherry Sauce (see Index), passed separately.

¼ cup rice
¾ cup sugar
3 cups milk
2 tablespoons gelatine
¾ cup cold water
¼ teaspoon mace
¼ teaspoon salt

1½ teaspoons vanilla
1½ teaspoons almond extract
1½ teaspoons rosewater
1 cup heavy cream
2 egg whites
Brandied Black Cherry Sauce
   (see Index)

YIELD: 10 servings

SOUFFLÉS

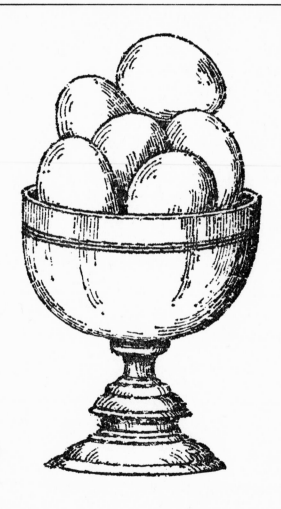

SOUFFLÉS

———◆———

Petits Soufflés à l'Orange, Oustau la Baumanière

Soufflé Jerez

Tartelettes Soufflées

Soufflé Normande (Apple Soufflé)

Coconut Soufflé Fado

Grinzinger Auflauf (Farina Soufflé)

Gesztenyekoch (Marron Soufflé)

Soufflé aux Pruneaux (Prune Soufflé)

Gräddkaka (Sour Cream Soufflé)

Petits Soufflés à l'Orange, Oustau la Baumanière

Oustau la Baumanière is a tiny hotel in Provence that boasts one of the top restaurants in all of France. The chef kindly invited me into his domain, and explained some details of dishes that I had inquired about. Though measuring cups are apparently unknown to him, and oven temperatures are gauged by hand rather than thermostat, his counsel has enabled me to produce some good facsimiles. You may prepare these *soufflés* ahead of time, up to the point where you beat the egg whites.

Preheat oven to 375°. In a saucepan, place ¼ cup flour and ½ cup sugar. Gradually add 2 cups of milk, and cook over low heat, stirring vigorously with a whisk, until thick. Remove from heat, add 8 egg yolks, replace over heat, and cook for a minute or so longer, or until very thick. (The mixture should reach the boiling point, but not boil.) Remove from heat again, add 1 teaspoon orange extract, ¼ cup very finely minced candied orange rind, and mix thoroughly. Beat 8 egg whites until stiff but not dry, fold into the egg-yolk mixture, and pour into 8 buttered 1½-cup *soufflé* dishes. (I use small casseroles.) Bake for 13 to 15 minutes. (The lesser time yields a more moist *soufflé*.)

¼ cup flour	1 teaspoon orange extract
½ cup sugar	¼ cup very finely minced candied orange rind
2 cups milk	
8 egg yolks	8 egg whites

YIELD: 8 servings

Soufflé Jerez

"Sherry" is a distortion of "Jerez." The English found it difficult to pronounce the name of this town in the heart of the sherry country in Spain, and so, over the years, "Jerez" became "sherry." This *soufflé* is denser than most, and filling; serve it after a light main course.

Marinate ¼ cup seeded raisins in 2 tablespoons sweet sherry for 2 hours. Preheat oven to 425°. In a saucepan, over low heat, melt 3 tablespoons butter. Stirring with a whisk, blend in ¼ cup flour. Gradually add 1 cup hot milk, and cook, stirring constantly, until thick. Remove from heat, and add ⅓ cup sugar, 4 egg yolks, ¼ cup walnuts, broken into small pieces, and the raisins and sherry. Mix well, fold in 2 whole ladyfingers and 3 Meringues (see Index), broken into several pieces each. (Buy meringues at a bakery, if you don't have any on hand. Generally, the bakery product is larger, so 2 will do.) Beat 5 egg whites until stiff but not dry, fold into the *soufflé* mixture, and pour into a well-buttered 8-inch *soufflé* dish. Bake for 20 to 25 minutes. (The shorter time will produce a more moist *soufflé*.) Serve with sweetened whipped cream, or ½ recipe Wine *Chaudeau* (see Index), substituting sweet sherry for Marsala wine.

¼ cup seeded raisins	2 whole ladyfingers
2 tablespoons sweet sherry	3 Meringues (see Index) or
3 tablespoons butter	2 bakery meringues
¼ cup flour	5 egg whites
1 cup hot milk	Sweetened whipped cream, or
⅓ cup sugar	½ recipe Wine *Chaudeau*
4 egg yolks	made with sherry (see In-
¼ cup walnuts	dex)

YIELD: 4 to 5 servings

Tartelettes Soufflées

Since these tart shells freeze very well, you would be wise to bake an extra supply, and store them in your freezer. Not only can you make these *souffléed* tarts in a matter of minutes, but you can fill them with fresh berries topped with a rosette of whipped cream, or with Napoleon Filling (see Index). They defrost in a few minutes at room temperature.

Preheat oven to 350°. Press 1 recipe Tart Dough (see Index) on the bottom and sides of 12 greased fluted tins, 4 inches in diameter and ¾ inch high. (Those I use are imported from France, and are generally available in well-stocked houseware departments. You may substitute metal or foil individual pie plates.) Prick the dough with a fork, and bake for 12 minutes, or until pale gold. Remove from pie plates, and cool.

In a bowl, mix 6 egg yolks, 6 tablespoons apricot jam, and 3 tablespoons of sugar. Add 12 almond macaroons, crumbled, and let the mixture stand for ½ hour or longer, until it may be mashed to a paste. (Preparation up to this point may be done in advance.)

Twenty-five minutes before servingtime, preheat oven to 350°. Beat 6 egg whites until stiff but not dry, and fold into macaroon mixture. Place tart shells on a baking sheet, fill with soufflé mixture, and bake for 11 to 12 minutes. With a pancake turner, carefully remove to individual plates, and serve immediately.

1 recipe Tart Dough (see Index)	3 tablespoons sugar
	12 almond macaroons
6 egg yolks	6 egg whites
6 tablespoons apricot jam	

YIELD: 12 servings

Soufflé Normande

Peel and core 2 small apples. Slice very thinly into a saucepan, sprinkle with 2 tablespoons sugar, cover, and cook over low heat until apples are tender. Uncover, and cook until apple slices are golden.

Preheat oven to 400°. In another saucepan, mix ⅔ cup sugar, ⅓ cup flour, ⅓ teaspoon salt, and 5 egg yolks. Gradually add 1⅔ cups milk, and stir until smooth. Cook over low heat, stirring constantly, until the mixture is very thick. (Do not permit it to boil.) Remove from heat, add 1 teaspoon orange extract, ⅓ cup Calvados, and 5 additional egg yolks. Beat 5 egg whites until stiff but not dry, and fold into the custard. Butter a deep 8-inch *soufflé* dish, dust with sugar, and pour in half the *soufflé* mixture. Arrange half the cooked apples on top, sprinkle with 5 almond macaroons, coarsely crumbled, and cover with remaining *soufflé*. Place remaining apples on top, bake for ½ hour, and serve immediately.

2 small apples	1⅔ cups milk
2 tablespoons sugar	1 teaspoon orange extract
⅔ cup sugar	⅓ cup Calvados
⅓ cup flour	5 egg yolks
⅓ teaspoon salt	5 egg whites
5 egg yolks	5 almond macaroons

YIELD: 6 servings

Coconut *Soufflé Fado*

Some of the finest *soufflés* I have eaten were served to me in
Portugal. This one was unexpectedly good, since I was taken
to a tiny restaurant primarily to hear the native *fado* singing.
The recipe was given to me mainly in sign language, and I
have had to reconstruct it.

Preheat oven to 350°. In a saucepan, over low heat, melt 3
tablespoons of butter. Add ¼ cup flour, and stir with a whisk
until smooth and bubbling. Gradually add 1 cup of hot milk,
and cook, stirring constantly, until the sauce is thick. Remove
from heat, add ⅓ cup sugar, 1 teaspoon vanilla, 4 egg yolks,
and 1 cup of flaked coconut. Beat 4 egg whites until stiff but
not dry, fold into coconut mixture, and pour into a greased
8-inch *soufflé* dish. Place in a pan filled to a depth of 1 inch
with hot water, and bake for 45 to 50 minutes. Serve immediately with Chocolate Sauce #2 (see Index).

3 tablespoons butter	1 teaspoon vanilla
¼ cup flour	4 egg yolks
1 cup hot milk	1 cup flaked coconut
⅓ cup sugar	4 egg whites

YIELD: 5 to 6 servings

Grinzinger Auflauf (Farina *Soufflé*)

The Viennese make all sorts of things with farina, including
soufflés.

Preheat oven to 325°. In a saucepan, combine ¼ cup farina,
a 2-inch piece of vanilla bean, and 2 cups of scalded milk.
Cook over low heat, stirring constantly, for 5 minutes, or until

thick. Remove from heat, discard the vanilla bean, and cool to lukewarm. Stir in ¼ cup sugar and 3 egg yolks. Beat 3 egg whites until stiff but not dry, fold into the farina mixture, and pour into a buttered 7-inch *soufflé* dish. Bake for 55 minutes, and serve immediately with Vanilla Sauce (see Index), Brandied Black Cherry Sauce (see Index), or Wine *Chaudeau* (see Index) passed separately.

¼ cup farina
2-inch piece of vanilla bean
2 cups scalded milk
¼ cup sugar
3 egg yolks

3 egg whites
Vanilla Sauce (see Index), Brandied Black Cherry Sauce (see Index), or Wine *Chaudeau* (see Index)

YIELD: 6 servings

Gesztenyekoch

Chestnuts are widely used throughout Europe both as a vegetable, and as a dessert ingredient. This Hungarian *soufflé* is an example of the latter.

Preheat oven to 425°. In a saucepan, mix ⅓ cup sugar, ¼ teaspoon salt, and ¼ cup flour. Gradually add 1 cup plus 1 tablespoon milk, and stir (preferably with a whisk) until smooth. Cook over low heat, stirring constantly, until thickened. Remove from heat, and add ½ cup Grand Marnier and 5 lightly beaten egg yolks. Return to heat and cook a minute more, or until thickened. (Do not permit it to boil.) Remove from heat once again. Drain the contents of a 9½-ounce jar of marrons in heavy syrup. Break each marron into 2 or 3 pieces, and fold into the hot custard. Beat 5 egg whites until stiff but not dry, and fold into the custard. Pour into a buttered and sugared 8-inch *soufflé* dish. Bake for 25 minutes (for a rather moist soufflé; a few minutes more if you like it dry).

Dust the top generously with confectioners' sugar. Heat ¼ cup
Grand Marnier, ignite, and pour blazing over the *soufflé*. Pass
the following sauce separately: To 1 recipe Vanilla Sauce (see
Index), add ¼ cup Grand Marnier, and fold in ½ cup heavy
cream, whipped until stiff.

⅓ cup sugar	5 egg whites
¼ teaspoon salt	Confectioners' sugar
¼ cup flour	¼ cup Grand Marnier
1 cup plus 1 tablespoon milk	1 recipe Vanilla Sauce (see
½ cup Grand Marnier	Index)
5 egg yolks	¼ cup Grand Marnier
1 9½-ounce jar marrons in	½ cup heavy cream
heavy syrup	

YIELD: 4 to 5 servings

Soufflé aux Pruneaux (Prune Soufflé)

Preheat oven to 350°. Finely chop enough large, cooked, pitted
prunes to yield 1 cup of pulp. (The largest size are best because they are the meatiest; about 12 should be enough. To
save time, you may use canned prunes.) Add 1 teaspoon almond extract, ¼ teaspoon cinnamon, and ¼ cup sugar. Beat
4 egg whites until foamy, add ¼ teaspoon cream of tartar, and
continue beating until stiff. Gently fold into the prune mixture.
Pour into a buttered and sugared 8-inch *soufflé* dish, and place
in a pan filled to a depth of 1 inch with hot water. Bake for 30
to 35 minutes. Serve immediately. Pass the sauce separately.

While the *soufflé* is baking, prepare the sauce. In a heat-
proof bowl or in the top of a double boiler beat 4 egg yolks,
¼ cup sugar, ½ teaspoon almond extract, and ⅔ cup prune
juice. Place over a pot of simmering water (the water must not
touch the bottom of the bowl), and beat vigorously with a

whisk or eggbeater until the sauce is thick and fluffy. Remove from heat and allow the bowl to cool for 2 or 3 minutes, then place over cracked ice (in a larger bowl), and continue beating until the sauce is cool and thick.

1 cup prune pulp (about 12 large prunes, cooked and chopped)	4 egg whites
	¼ teaspoon cream of tartar
	4 egg yolks
1 teaspoon almond extract	¼ cup sugar
¼ teaspoon cinnamon	½ teaspoon almond extract
¼ cup sugar	⅔ cup prune juice

YIELD: 4 servings

Gräddkaka (Sour Cream Soufflé)

Soufflés may be mixed an hour before bakingtime; pour into the soufflé dish, and cover. At bakingtime, uncover and place in the oven. Serve this Scandinavian cream soufflé plain or with Brandied Black Cherry Sauce (see Index).

Preheat oven to 350°. Beat 3 egg yolks with ⅓ cup sugar until thick and light. Beat in 6 tablespoons flour and the grated rind of 1 lemon. Fold in 1½ cups of sour cream, and lastly, 3 stiffly beaten egg whites. Pour into a buttered and sugared 7- or 8-inch soufflé dish, and bake for 35 minutes. Dust generously with confectioners' sugar, and serve immediately.

3 egg yolks	1½ cups sour cream
⅓ cup sugar	3 egg whites
6 tablespoons flour	Confectioners' sugar
Grated rind of 1 lemon	

YIELD: 4 servings

REFRIGERATOR AND
FROZEN DESSERTS

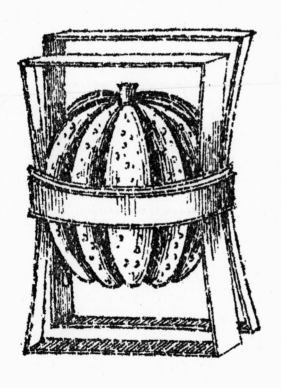

ICE CREAMS AND MOUSSES, COLD *SOUFFLÉS*

———◆————

Cassata Elena (Frozen Icebox Cake)

Mousse de Fraises, Framboise (Strawberry Mousse)

Soufflé Glacé au Chocolat (Frozen Chocolate *Soufflé*)

Timbale Elysées (Ice Cream-Filled Pastry Shells)

Dutch Chocolate Frozen Pudding

Les Dentelles de Lucie
(Lace Cookies with Ice Cream and Rum Sauce)

Frozen Cream *Oporto* (Frozen Wine Cream)

Soufflé Glacé Baur au Lac (Frozen Grand Marnier *Soufflé*)

Cassata Elena (Frozen Icebox Cake)

Split 15 ladyfingers in half lengthwise, and dip the cut sides quickly into 2 tablespoons Marsala wine. Lightly butter the inside of a 1-quart baking dish or mold, and line it with the ladyfingers, rounded side out. (To give the finished *cassata* a good appearance, stand the ladyfingers around the sides upright; the butter will hold them in place.) Beat 6 egg yolks with ½ cup sugar until thick and light. Stir in ¼ cup Marsala wine, 2 ounces of dark sweet chocolate, chopped, and ¼ cup toasted slivered almonds. Fold in ¾ cup heavy cream, whipped, and pour into lined mold. Place in the freezer for 5 hours.

Insert a sharp knife around the inside of the mold to loosen edges and turn out onto a platter. Decorate with ½ cup heavy cream, whipped until stiff with 1 tablespoon sugar. (An attractive way to decorate it is to put the cream in a pastry bag fitted with a star tube, and force out the cream in vertical lines between the upright ladyfingers.)

15 ladyfingers	2 ounces dark sweet chocolate, chopped
2 tablespoons Marsala wine	¼ cup toasted slivered almonds
Butter	¾ cup heavy cream
6 egg yolks	½ cup heavy cream
½ cup sugar	1 tablespoon sugar
¼ cup Marsala wine	

YIELD: 6 servings

Mousse de Fraises, Framboise
(Strawberry Mousse)

Try this with other berries or puréed fruits instead of strawberries; remember to change the liqueur to suit the fruit.

In the top of a double boiler, over medium heat, heat 1⅓ cups of sweetened condensed milk for 5 minutes. Cool in the freezer for 10 minutes. Pour into the small bowl of the electric mixer and beat at high speed for 5 minutes. Fold in 1 cup puréed fresh strawberries, 3 tablespoons Framboise liqueur, and 1 cup heavy cream, whipped. Freeze mixture until about ¼ inch around edge has become firm; then beat until smooth. Pour into a 1-quart mold and freeze 4 to 5 hours, or until firm. Run tip of a sharp knife around inside of mold to loosen mousse. Dip mold into a pan of hot water for a few seconds. Turn out mousse onto a platter and keep in freezer until servingtime. (If there is too long an interval and mousse is too hard, remove from freezer a few minutes before.) Surround mousse with 1 quart large, ripe, unhulled strawberries.

1⅛ cups sweetened condensed milk
1 cup puréed fresh strawberries
3 tablespoons Framboise liqueur

1 cup heavy cream
1 quart large ripe strawberries

YIELD: 6 servings

Soufflé Glacé au Chocolat
(Frozen Chocolate Soufflé)

This recipe is from the Tour d'Argent in Paris.

In a small saucepan, over low heat, stirring constantly, melt 1 cup chocolate bits in 1 cup water. Add ½ cup confectioners' sugar and continue to cook and stir until sugar is dissolved. Remove from heat, add 1 teaspoon vanilla, and cool. Beat ¾ cup heavy cream until stiff, and fold into the chocolate mixture. Pour into small dessert dishes or *pots de crème*. Freeze 1½ to 2 hours before serving.

1 cup chocolate bits
1 cup water
½ cup confectioners' sugar

1 teaspoon vanilla
¾ cup heavy cream

YIELD: 6 servings

Timbale Elysées (Ice Cream-Filled Pastry Shells)

As this recipe was originally given to me, it was a great deal more elaborate. It involved making *génoise* (for which I substitute ladyfingers), and individual domes of spun sugar to crown each *timbale*. Since I have often served this streamlined version with great success, I trust that the chef at the Lasserre Restaurant in Paris who gave me the recipe will forgive my taking liberties with his creation.

Preheat oven to 375°. In the small bowl of the electric mixer, beat 1 egg, ⅔ of an extra egg white, and ⅓ cup sugar until thick and light. (When I have leftover egg whites, I freeze them singly in plastic cups. When frozen, remove from cup, place in a plastic bag, and store in freezer. In a warm place they defrost in about 10 minutes.) Beat in ⅔ cup flour. Spoon 2 tablespoons batter on one end of a well-greased baking sheet, and, with the back of a spoon, spread to a 4½- to 5-inch circle. (The thinner you spread the batter, the better the result.) Repeat at the other end of the sheet, and bake for 4 minutes, or until the circles begin to show golden brown around the edges. Remove from the sheet immediately, place a circle over the top of an inverted custard cup, and, with your hands, press wafer against the cup. In a few seconds, it will stiffen in a cup shape. Remove from cup, and repeat with second wafer. If the second wafer has already stiffened, replace in oven for a few seconds to soften. Repeat with remaining batter; you will have 6 to 8 cups.

Shortly before servingtime, prepare the following: Whip ¾ cup heavy cream until stiff; cut 4 ladyfingers in half, lengthwise, break each half in two, and sprinkle with 2 tablespoons kirsch; soften ⅓ cup currant jelly; prepare 1½ cups diced fresh fruit or berries in season.

At servingtime, place 2 pieces of ladyfinger and some of the fruit in the bottom of each pastry cup, place a large scoop of vanilla ice cream on top, spread with currant jelly, and top with a rosette of the whipped cream, pressed through a pastry tube. Decorate with candied rose petals or violets.

A very elegant, turn-of-the-century dessert, and, once you have everything set out, not hard to prepare! You may bake the pastry cups a day or so ahead, and store in a tin, or, make them well ahead, and freeze.

1 egg	2 tablespoons kirsch
⅔ of an extra egg white	⅓ cup currant jelly
⅓ cup sugar	1½ cups diced fresh fruit or
⅔ cup flour	berries
¾ cup heavy cream	Vanilla ice cream
4 ladyfingers	Candied rose petals or violets

YIELD: 6 to 8 servings

Dutch Chocolate Frozen Pudding

In the top of a double boiler, cook 1 cup milk, 1 tablespoon quick-cooking tapioca, and 1 ounce bitter chocolate (preferably Dutch chocolate), for 10 minutes. Remove from heat, add 1 egg yolk mixed with ½ cup sugar, ⅛ teaspoon powdered cloves, and ½ teaspoon cinnamon. Replace over heat, and cook for 1 minute longer. Cool for 5 minutes, and fold in 1 egg white, beaten until stiff. Chill in refrigerator or freezer.

Plump ¼ cup dark raisins in hot water for 15 minutes, and

drain. To the cold chocolate mixture, add the drained raisins, ¼ cup strained raspberry jam, ⅓ cup walnuts, broken into small pieces, and 2 tablespoons minced candied cherries. Fold in 1 cup of heavy cream, whipped until stiff, and pour into a 5-cup mold. Freeze for 8 hours, or until firm. To serve, dip the mold into hot water for a few seconds, and turn out onto a platter. Sprinkle with shaved bitter chocolate.

1 cup milk	1 egg white
1 tablespoon quick-cooking tapioca	¼ cup dark raisins
	¼ cup strained raspberry jam
1 ounce bitter chocolate	⅓ cup walnuts
1 egg yolk	2 tablespoons minced candied cherries
½ cup sugar	
⅛ teaspoon powdered cloves	1 cup heavy cream
½ teaspoon cinnamon	Shaved bitter chocolate

YIELD: 8 servings

Les Dentelles de Lucie
(Lace Cookies with Ice Cream and Rum Sauce)

The crisp toffee-colored wafers that are the base for this dessert are lacy and delicate, a good foil for ice cream. One word of caution: In humid weather, they lose their crispness quickly. Keep them in the freezer if you bake them more than an hour before servingtime. They defrost in less than a minute.

Preheat oven to 350°. In a small saucepan, heat ¼ pound butter, ½ cup sugar, ¾ cup ground hazelnuts, 1 tablespoon flour, and 2 tablespoons cream, until the butter melts. On an ungreased baking sheet, drop 4 evenly-spaced mounds of batter (1 tablespoon each), and bake for 10 minutes. Leave the wafers on the pan for a minute or so until they become stiff enough to remove with a broad spatula. Repeat with the remaining batter.

At servingtime, put 1 wafer on each dessert plate, and top with a scoop of vanilla ice cream. Make a double recipe of Rum Sauce (see Index), dribble a little over the ice cream, and pass the remaining sauce separately in a sauceboat.

¼ pound butter	2 tablespoons cream
½ cup sugar	About 3 pints vanilla ice cream
¾ cup ground hazelnuts	Double recipe Rum Sauce (see
1 tablespoon flour	Index)

YIELD: 16 servings

Frozen Cream *Oporto* (Frozen Wine Cream)

Bake a double recipe of Meringues (see Index), or buy 12 medium-size meringues from a bakery. Whip 2 cups of heavy cream until stiff with ⅔ cup sugar. Fold in ¼ cup Port wine and the Meringues broken into fairly small pieces (about the size of a quarter). Rinse a 2-quart mold or loaf tin with cold water, pour in the cream mixture, and freeze for 6 hours or until firm. Run the tip of a sharp knife around the inside of the mold to loosen the cream, dip the mold into hot water for a few seconds, and turn out onto a serving platter. Purée 1 pint of strawberries, raspberries, or peeled, sliced fresh peaches, sweeten to taste, and pass this sauce separately, or serve with Brandied Black Cherry Sauce (see Index).

Double recipe of Meringues (see Index) or 12 purchased meringues	1 pint strawberries, raspberries, or sliced fresh peaches, sweetened
2 cups heavy cream	*or*
⅔ cup sugar	Brandied Black Cherry Sauce
¼ cup Port wine	(see Index)

YIELD: 10 to 12 servings

Soufflé Glacé Baur au Lac
(Frozen Grand Marnier *Soufflé*)

The cuisine at the Baur au Lac in Zurich earns and enjoys a fine reputation. The menu is continental rather than limited to Swiss specialties. Whether or not I need 12 servings of frozen soufflé, I make the full recipe; it keeps admirably in the freezer for 3 or 4 weeks.

In a small bowl, mix 10 almond macaroons, crumbled, 3 tablespoons Grand Marnier, and 2 tablespoons orange juice. Mash to a paste. Separate 5 eggs, reserving 4 of the whites. Beat the 5 egg yolks with ⅔ cup sugar until very thick and light. Stir in 3 tablespoons Grand Marnier and the grated rind of 1 orange. Fold in 2 cups of heavy cream, whipped until stiff, and the 4 egg whites, beaten until stiff but not dry. Pour half the mixture into 12 custard cups, spoon some of the macaroon paste on top of the batter, and cover with the remaining cream mixture. Freeze for 4 hours, or until firm.

At servingtime, unmold onto individual dessert plates. Sift ¼ teaspoon cocoa on top of each soufflé, and pour 1 tablespoon Grand Marnier around each. Pass the bottle of Grand Marnier for those who wish additional liqueur.

10 almond macaroons	3 tablespoons Grand Marnier
3 tablespoons Grand Marnier	Grated rind of 1 orange
2 tablespoons orange juice	2 cups heavy cream
5 eggs	1 tablespoon cocoa
⅔ cup sugar	¾ cup Grand Marnier

YIELD: 12 servings

ICEBOX CAKES

Dolce Freddo alla Cioccolata (Chocolate Icebox Mold)

Charlotte aux Poires au Chocolat
(Pear and Chocolate Icebox Cake)

Charlotte Russe

Mullvad (Icebox Cake with Prunes)

Boule de Neige (Snowball)

Berghof Icebox Cake

Belmouth House Summer Dessert

Le Mieux (Marron Icebox Cake)

Fantasia di Francesca (Fruit Macaroon Icebox Cake)

Dolce Freddo alla Cioccolata
(Chocolate Icebox Mold)

In the bowl of the electric mixer, beat until fluffy: 1 egg, 1 egg yolk, ¾ cup sweet butter, 1½ cups confectioners' sugar, 1 teaspoon each almond extract and vanilla, and ½ cup cocoa. Fold in 1½ cups ground almonds and 32 Social Teas or Arrowroot biscuits, broken into 6 to 8 pieces each. Spoon into a buttered 1-quart mold or small loaf tin, and refrigerate for 6 hours or overnight.

Run the tip of a sharp knife around the inside of the mold, dip mold in hot water for ½ minute, and invert onto serving platter. Sprinkle with ¼ cup chopped, toasted almonds, and refrigerate until servingtime. Serve in thin slices with sweetened whipped cream, or Vanilla Cream (see Index), passed separately.

1 egg
1 egg yolk
¾ cup sweet butter
1½ cups confectioners' sugar
1 teaspoon almond extract
1 teaspoon vanilla
½ cup cocoa

1½ cups ground almonds
32 Social Teas or Arrowroot
   biscuits
¼ cup chopped toasted almonds
Sweetened whipped cream or
   Vanilla Cream (see Index)
YIELD: 8 servings

Charlotte aux Poires au Chocolat
(Pear and Chocolate Icebox Cake)

This is essentially a chocolate mousse, but the addition of ladyfingers and fruit renders it lighter, and happily, less caloric. If that is not your concern, you may eliminate the ladyfingers and pears, and serve it in parfait glasses or *pots de crème,* but you will have 7 or 8 servings instead of 10.

Lightly butter the inside of a 1½-quart mold, and line it with 20 ladyfingers, split in half lengthwise. Stand them upright around the sides, placing them rounded side out. In the top of a double boiler, melt 5 ounces of semisweet chocolate, and 2½ ounces of bitter chocolate, in 1 tablespoon milk. Remove from heat, add ¾ cup sugar, and 5 egg yolks, and beat until smooth. Peel, core, and dice 3 firm medium-size pears, and fold into chocolate mixture. Beat 5 egg whites until stiff but not dry, and fold into chocolate. Pour into lined mold, and chill for 4 hours. Invert onto serving platter.

20 ladyfingers	¾ cup sugar
5 ounces semisweet chocolate	5 egg yolks
2½ ounces bitter chocolate	3 firm, medium-size pears
1 tablespoon milk	5 egg whites

YIELD: 10 servings

Charlotte Russe

This is a truly gala dessert; consequently I like to give this recipe in terms of 16 to 20 servings. It is Viennese in origin; from the Vienna that knew a gay, ebullient and splendid way of life.

Make the filling first: In the top of a double boiler, cook 14 ounces semisweet chocolate, 1½ cups Vanilla Sugar (see Index), and 1½ cups light cream, until the chocolate is melted. In a mixing bowl, beat 8 eggs lightly, stir in the chocolate mixture, pour back into the top of the double boiler, and cook until thickened, stirring occasionally. (Adding the chocolate mixture to the eggs in the bowl is a safeguard against curdling.

This might happen if you poured the eggs directly into the top of the double boiler, where the temperature is so much higher.) While the mixture cooks, soak 2 tablespoons of gelatine in ⅓ cup of cold water. When the chocolate mixture is thick, remove from the heat, add the soaked gelatine, and stir until gelatine dissolves. Cool completely.

While the filling cools, make a Jelly Roll. (You may substitute a purchased jelly roll, but I prefer the texture of a home-made one.) Preheat oven to 400°. Grease an 11-by-17-inch jelly-roll pan, line with waxed paper, grease the paper thoroughly, and dust with sugar. Beat 4 egg whites until foamy, gradually add ¼ cup sugar, continuing to beat until the meringue is stiff and glossy. In a separate bowl beat 4 egg yolks with ¼ cup sugar until thick and light. Alternately, fold the meringue and ⅔ cup sifted flour into the yolk mixture. Spread the cake mixture in the prepared tin, and bake for 12 minutes, or until the cake starts to shrink from the sides of the tin. (Do not overbake the cake, or it may get too crisp to roll.) Immediately, turn roll out onto a piece of waxed paper, peel off top paper and, starting from the long side, roll up the cake. Unroll immediately, spread with 1 cup raspberry jam, roll up again, and cool. Cut the roll into slices ¼ inch thick, and line the bottom and sides of a 9- or 10-inch spring-form pan or a 3-quart bowl with the slices.

Into the cooled chocolate mixture, fold 3 cups heavy cream, whipped until stiff. Pick out the cherries from two 12-ounce jars of Bing cherry preserves, and fold the fruit into the filling. Pour filling into the cake-lined bowl or pan, and trim off any pieces of cake that may extend higher than the filling. Cover the filling with these pieces and with any slices of jelly roll you may have left over. Chill the cake for 6 hours, or until firm.

Run the tip of a sharp knife around the inside of mold to loosen edges, and invert cake onto serving platter. Whip ½

cup heavy cream until stiff, and decorate the cake with
rosettes of cream forced through a pastry tube. Whip 1 cup
heavy cream until stiff, stir in ½ cup syrup from the cherry
preserves, and pass this sauce separately.

14 ounces semisweet chocolate	4 egg yolks
1½ cups Vanilla Sugar (see Index)	¼ cup sugar
	⅔ cup sifted flour
1½ cups light cream	1 cup raspberry jam
8 eggs	3 cups heavy cream
2 tablespoons gelatine	2 12-ounce jars Bing cherry pre-
⅓ cup cold water	serves
4 egg whites	½ cup heavy cream
¼ cup sugar	1 cup heavy cream

YIELD: 16 to 20 servings

Mullvad (Icebox Cake with Prunes)

Mullvad translated from Swedish means mole, certainly a
strange name for a perfectly delicious icebox cake. When you
learn that *Mullvad* contains prunes, hidden under a layer of
cream, the reason behind the name becomes more obvious.
Nevertheless, I do not enlighten the uninitiated beforehand;
this is one case where the rose-by-any-other-name theory has
been carried too far!

Cook ¾ pound of extra large prunes (about 24), in water to
cover, until tender. Drain and cool the prunes, and remove
pits. Replace each pit with a piece of candied orange rind. In a
small saucepan, soak 1 tablespoon gelatine in ⅓ cup cold water
for 5 minutes, then heat slowly until gelatine is dissolved. Remove from heat, and cool. Beat 2 eggs with ⅔ cup sugar until
thick and light, add cooled gelatine, and stir until blended.
Beat 2½ cups heavy cream until stiff, fold half the cream into

the gelatine mixture, and reserve the rest. Place the custard cream and reserved whipped cream in the refrigerator.

Split 20 ladyfingers in half, lengthwise. Lightly butter the inside of a 9-inch spring-form pan. Line the bottom and sides of the form with the ladyfingers. (Around the sides, stand them upright, rounded side out.) Cover the bottom layer of ladyfingers with the prunes, and pour the custard cream over them. Spoon the reserved whipped cream into a pastry tube fitted with a star opening, and press out the cream in rosettes over the top of the cake. Chill for several hours until firm. Remove sides of pan, and, with a sharp knife, loosen the cake from the bottom. Slide cake onto a serving platter, and replace in the refrigerator until servingtime.

You may substitute other cooked, drained fruit for the prunes, but do try this combination; it's unusual and unusually good.

¾ pound extra large prunes	2 eggs
Candied orange rind	⅔ cup sugar
1 tablespoon gelatine	2½ cups heavy cream
⅓ cup water	20 ladyfingers

YIELD: 10 to 12 servings

Boule de Neige (Snowball)

Boule de Neige, or Snowball, is generally made with ice cream. My good friend Alvin Kerr, food and wine consultant, magazine columnist, and gastronome, created his own version. It is spectacular to look at; I have seen it. It is delicious to eat; I have enjoyed it more than once.

Preheat oven to 325°. Lightly grease two 3-cup ovenproof mixing bowls, line them with waxed paper, and grease the paper. Beat 6 egg yolks with ½ cup sugar until thick and lemon-colored. Stir in ½ teaspoon vanilla, 1 teaspoon lemon juice, and the grated rind of ½ lemon. Fold in 1 cup sifted cake flour. Beat 6 egg whites with ¼ teaspoon salt until stiff but not dry, and fold into the yolk mixture. Pour ½ the batter into each prepared bowl, and bake for 40 minutes, or until the top springs back when pressed gently. Invert the bowls on a rack, and leave until the cakes are cool.

Remove the cakes from the bowls, peel off the paper, and cut a slice from the top of each cake, so that when the cakes are put together they form a sphere. Cut a thin slice from the bottom of one cake, to form a base. Carefully cut out some of the inside of each cake, leaving shells 1 inch thick.

While the cake is baking, prepare the filling. Marinate ¼ cup finely ground candied fruits in 2 tablespoons kirsch for 1 hour. Soak 1½ teaspoons gelatine in 2 tablespoons cold water. In the top of a double boiler, combine 2 egg yolks and ¼ cup sugar, and beat with a wooden spoon until the mixture is smooth and creamy. Gradually stir in ½ cup hot light cream, and cook over hot water, stirring constantly, until the cream thickens. Add the softened gelatine, and stir until it is completely dissolved. Cool the cream, stirring occasionally. When it is cold, stir in the fruit with its marinade, then fold in ¾ cup heavy cream, whipped until stiff.

Sprinkle 1 teaspoon kirsch on the inside of each cake shell, fill with the cream, and refrigerate until set. Put the shells together, forming a sphere, and place on a serving platter. Whip 1½ cups heavy cream until stiff with 1 tablespoon sugar and 1 teaspoon cognac. Spoon into a pastry tube fitted with a star nozzle, and pipe rosettes over the entire surface of the cake sphere. Chill in the refrigerator for 6 hours, or in the freezer for 2 hours. Decorate the top of the cake with 6 crystallized violets, and arrange crystallized mint leaves around the base. Serve the *Boule de Neige* in wedge-shaped cuts.

6 egg yolks
½ cup sugar
½ teaspoon vanilla
1 teaspoon lemon juice
Grated rind of ½ lemon
1 cup sifted cake flour
6 egg whites
¼ teaspoon salt
¼ cup finely ground candied
  fruits
2 tablespoons kirsch
1½ teaspoons gelatine

2 tablespoons cold water
2 egg yolks
¼ cup sugar
½ cup hot light cream
¾ cup heavy cream
1 teaspoon kirsch
1½ cups heavy cream
1 tablespoon sugar
1 teaspoon cognac
6 crystallized violets
Crystallized mint leaves

YIELD: 8 servings

Berghof Icebox Cake

In a saucepan, bring to a boil 1 cup of water and 1¼ cups of sugar. Add 1 pound each sweet black cherries and sour cherries, both pitted, and simmer over medium heat for 10 minutes. Drain the cherries, reserving juices. (Or, use a 1-pound can of black cherries and a 1-pound can of red cherries, each in heavy syrup.)

Split 12 ladyfingers in half, lengthwise, and sprinkle each half with ¼ teaspoon kirsch. Line a loaf pan, approximately 5-by-9 inches, with waxed paper, and place 8 half-ladyfingers, rounded side down, in the bottom of the tin. In a saucepan, bring to a boil ½ cup milk and 1 cup ground almonds. Remove from heat, and cool. Cream ¼ pound sweet butter with ½ cup sugar until light and fluffy. Beat in 2 egg yolks, 1 tablespoon kirsch, and the cooled almond mixture. Spread half of this mixture over the ladyfingers in the pan, then cover with half the drained cherries. Repeat these layers, and cover with remaining ladyfingers. Refrigerate for 4 hours.

Meanwhile, make the sauce: For each cup of reserved cherry juice, blend in 1 teaspoon cornstarch. In a small saucepan, bring juice and cornstarch to a boil, and cook until slightly thickened and clear. Remove from heat, add 1 tablespoon kirsch, pour into a sauceboat, and chill.

When cake is chilled turn out onto a serving platter, and peel off the waxed paper. Whip 1 cup heavy cream until stiff with 2 tablespoons sugar and 1 teaspoon kirsch. With ¾ of the whipped cream, frost the top and sides of the cake. Spoon the remainder into a pastry tube fitted with a star-shaped opening, and pipe rosettes of cream in a decorative pattern on top of the cake. Chill until servingtime. Pass the sauce separately.

1 cup water	½ cup sugar
1¼ cups sugar	2 egg yolks
1 pound sweet black cherries	1 tablespoon kirsch
1 pound sour cherries	Cherry juice
12 ladyfingers	Cornstarch
2 tablespoons kirsch	1 tablespoon kirsch
½ cup milk	1 cup heavy cream
1 cup ground almonds	2 tablespoons sugar
¼ pound sweet butter	1 teaspoon kirsch

YIELD: 8 servings

Belmouth House Summer Dessert

Cook 1½ cups of stemmed currants with ½ cup sugar until the sugar is melted. Cook 1½ cups of hulled raspberries with ½ cup sugar until the sugar is melted. Cook 1½ cups of stemmed and tailed gooseberries with ½ cup sugar until the berries are just tender. Keep all the berries hot.

Trim the crusts from 16 slices of raisin bread, and spread the bread with 6 tablespoons of sweet butter, softened. Cover the bottom of a loaf pan with the bread, buttered side up. Spread the hot currants on the bread, and pour on the juice. Repeat the bread layer, and cover with the raspberries and raspberry juice. Again repeat the bread layer, and cover with gooseberries and gooseberry juice. Finish with a layer of bread, buttered side down. Cover with a piece of foil, weight the top (one or two cans make a good weight), and chill for 5 hours. Shortly before servingtime, remove the weights and the foil, turn out onto a serving platter, and frost the top and sides of the dessert with ¾ cup heavy cream, whipped until stiff, with 2 tablespoons sugar.

1½ cups stemmed currants	½ cup sugar
½ cup sugar	16 slices raisin bread
1½ cups raspberries	6 tablespoons sweet butter
½ cup sugar	¾ cup heavy cream
1½ cups stemmed and tailed gooseberries	2 tablespoons sugar
	YIELD: 6 to 8 servings

Le Mieux (Marron Icebox Cake)

Whoever dreamed up this icebox cake suffered not a whit from false modesty. He called it simply *Le Mieux*, The Best.

Cut a bakery pound cake into ¼-inch-thick slices (or bake ½ recipe Tartan Tea Cake [see Index] or Pound Cake [see Index], in a smaller tin; reduce baking time about 10 minutes). Line the bottom and sides of a lightly buttered 9-inch spring-form pan with some of the sliced cake. Soak 1 tablespoon gelatine in ¼ cup cold water. Drain a 9½-ounce jar of marrons in heavy syrup. Measure half the syrup into a saucepan. Separate 5 eggs, reserving 4 of the whites. To the syrup, add 3 tablespoons sugar and the 5 egg yolks. Blend with a whisk, then add 1¼ cups hot milk. Cook over low heat, beating constantly with the whisk, until the custard thickens. (Do not allow it to boil.)

Remove from heat, add the soaked gelatine, and stir until the gelatine is dissolved. Add ¼ cup Benedictine and Brandy (or 2 tablespoons each cognac and any fruit liqueur). Coarsely chop the drained marrons, and add half to the custard with 6 almond macaroons, crumbled. (Reserve the remaining marrons.) Chill the custard. When it is on the point of setting, fold in the 4 egg whites, stiffly beaten. Spoon a portion of the custard into the lined spring-form pan. Cover with a layer of the sliced pound cake. Repeat these layers until cake and custard are used up. (The top should be a custard layer.) Chill until set.

While the cake is setting, hull, wash, and drain 1½ pints of strawberries. (You may substitute two 1-pound cans of peaches or cherries, pitted and drained.) Whip 2 cups heavy cream until stiff. Unmold the chilled cake onto a serving platter. Frost the sides with ⅓ of the whipped cream. Dip the strawberries into ½ cup currant jelly that has been melted and cooled, and place them on top of the cake. Fold the reserved marrons into the remaining whipped cream. Add marron syrup to taste, and spoon into a serving bowl. Chill the cake and sauce until servingtime.

Bakery pound cake
1 tablespoon gelatine
¼ cup cold water
1 9½-ounce jar of marrons in heavy syrup
3 tablespoons sugar
5 eggs
1¼ cups hot milk

¼ cup Benedictine and Brandy
6 almond macaroons
1½ pints strawberries, or two 1-pound cans peaches or cherries
2 cups heavy cream
½ cup currant jelly, melted and cooled

YIELD: 12 to 16 servings

Fantasia di Francesca
(Fruit Macaroon Icebox Cake)

Preheat oven to 350°. Beat 1 egg with ¼ cup of sugar until thick and light. Sift together 2 tablespoons flour, 2 tablespoons potato flour, and ¼ teaspoon baking powder. Fold into the egg-sugar mixture, and pour into a greased 9-inch spring-form pan. Bake for 15 minutes, or until the top of the cake springs back when pressed lightly. Cool the cake in the pan. (You may substitute a 9-inch layer bought from a bakery: Slice in half horizontally, place one half, cut side down, into the pan. Reserve the other half for another use. If only 8-inch layers are available, slice in half, place one half, cut side down, into the pan, and cut pieces from the other half to fill in the spaces.)

Simmer 1 cup of dried apricots in water to cover for 10 minutes, or until just tender. Drain, cool, and cut into small pieces. Soak 2 tablespoons gelatine in ½ cup orange juice, dissolve over low heat, and cool.

Line the sides of the pan with a single row of almond macaroons, rounded side out (you will need about 13 macaroons). In the small bowl of the electric mixer, beat 3 eggs with 1 cup light brown sugar, packed, for 10 minutes, or until very thick and light. Finely mash enough bananas to yield 1 cup of pulp (about 2 large ones), and mix with the cooled gelatine. Fold in the egg-sugar mixture, and pour into the prepared pan. Chill until lightly set. Cover the top with the apricot pieces, spread with ¼ cup softened apricot jam, and sprinkle with ¼ cup chopped pistachio nuts. Chill for 3 hours.

Remove sides of pan, and place cake on a platter. Whip 1½ cups heavy cream until very stiff with ⅓ cup sugar. Spoon into a pastry tube fitted with a star-shaped opening, and pipe spiral mounds to cover the top of the cake. Pipe vertical lines on the sides of the cake between the macaroons, and tiny rosettes around the base. Sprinkle 1 tablespoon of very finely chopped pistachio nuts on top of the cake, and chill until servingtime.

1 egg	3 eggs
¼ cup sugar	1 cup light brown sugar, packed
2 tablespoons flour	2 to 3 large bananas
2 tablespoons potato flour	¼ cup apricot jam
¼ teaspoon baking powder	¼ cup chopped pistachio nuts
1 cup dried apricots	1½ cups heavy cream
2 tablespoons gelatine	⅓ cup sugar
½ cup orange juice	1 tablespoon very finely
About 13 almond macaroons	chopped pistachio nuts

YIELD: 12 to 14 servings

FROSTINGS,
FILLINGS, SAUCES

FROSTINGS, FILLINGS, SAUCES

Chocolate Butter Cream

Vanilla Sauce

Chocolate Sauce #1

Chocolate Sauce #2

Crème Pâtissière (Custard Fillings, see *Brioche aux Cerises,* p. 46)

Chocolate Frosting #1

Chocolate Frosting #2

Chocolate Frosting #3

Wine Chaudeau (see p. 175)

Rum Sauce

Cream Frosting

Napoleon Filling

Brandied Black Cherry Sauce

Vanilla Sugar and Confectioners' Vanilla **Sugar**

Ginger Hard Sauce
(see Baked Pears *Roosendaal,* p. 154)

Chocolate Butter Cream

In the top of a double boiler, melt 4 ounces of bitter chocolate. In a small saucepan, using a whisk, beat 2 eggs with 1½ cups of sugar until smooth. Cook over low heat, stirring constantly, for 3 minutes. Do not allow to boil, lest the eggs curdle. Remove from heat, add the melted chocolate, and ¾ pound of sweet butter, cut in small pieces. Stir until butter is dissolved and mixture is smooth. Refrigerate for 1 hour, or until of spreading consistency.

4 ounces bitter chocolate	1½ cups sugar
2 eggs	¾ pound sweet butter

YIELD: about 3½ cups

Vanilla Sauce

In a saucepan, mix 2 teaspoons cornstarch, ¼ cup Vanilla Sugar (see Index), and 3 egg yolks. Stir in 2¼ cups milk. Cook over low heat, stirring constantly, preferably with a whisk, until the mixture coats a spoon. Remove from heat and cool, stirring occasionally to prevent the formation of a skin.

2 teaspoons cornstarch	3 egg yolks
¼ cup Vanilla Sugar (see Index)	2¼ cups milk

YIELD: about 2⅓ cups

Chocolate Sauce #1

In a saucepan, put ¼ pound each bitter chocolate and milk chocolate, and 2 cups heavy cream. Cook over low heat, stirring constantly, until chocolate is melted. Add ¼ cup each honey and sugar, and 1 teaspoon cinnamon, and continue to cook, stirring, until sauce is of desired consistency.

¼ pound bitter chocolate   ¼ cup honey
¼ pound milk chocolate   ¼ cup sugar
2 cups heavy cream   1 teaspoon cinnamon
                    YIELD: about 3 cups

Chocolate Sauce #2

In a saucepan, over low heat, melt ½ pound milk chocolate in 1 cup light cream. Bring the mixture to a rolling boil, stirring constantly. Turn down the heat, and simmer the sauce until it thickens. Remove from heat, and stir in 2 tablespoons cognac.

½ pound milk chocolate   2 tablespoons cognac
1 cup light cream
                    YIELD: about 1¾ cups

Chocolate Frosting #1

In a small saucepan, mix 2 tablespoons butter, 3 tablespoons milk, ¾ cup sugar, 1 tablespoon light corn syrup, and 1 ounce bitter chocolate, chopped coarsely. Cook over medium heat, stirring constantly, until a drop forms a soft ball in cold water.

Remove from heat, stir in ½ teaspoon vanilla, and spread on cake immediately.

2 tablespoons butter
3 tablespoons milk
¾ cup sugar

1 tablespoon light corn syrup
1 ounce bitter chocolate
½ teaspoon vanilla

YIELD: Frosting for two 8-inch layers, or one 9-by-12-inch layer

Chocolate Frosting #2

In the top of a double boiler, heat 1½ cups chocolate bits, ½ cup strong coffee, and 2 tablespoons butter, until butter and chocolate are melted. Remove from heat, and beat until smooth and of spreading consistency.

1½ cups chocolate bits
½ cup strong coffee

2 tablespoons butter

YIELD: about 1⅛ cups; enough to cover top and sides of two 8- or 9-inch layers

Chocolate Frosting #3

As you know, most chocolate frostings acquire a gray, spotted look once they have been refrigerated; this one doesn't!

In the top of a double boiler, cook 1 cup chocolate bits, ¼ cup light corn syrup, and 2 tablespoons strong coffee, water, or rum, until the chocolate is melted. Spread on cake while frosting is warm.

1 cup chocolate bits
¼ cup light corn syrup

2 tablespoons strong coffee, water, or rum

YIELD: frosting for two 9-inch layers, top and sides

Rum Sauce

In a saucepan, mix 1½ cups light brown sugar, 3 tablespoons sweet butter, and ½ cup light cream. Over medium heat, stirring constantly, bring to the boiling point. Turn up heat and boil briskly for 3 minutes, or until sauce thickens. Remove from heat, set aside for 3 minutes, then stir in 2 tablespoons light rum. Serve warm or cold.

1½ cups light brown sugar	½ cup light cream
3 tablespoons sweet butter	2 tablespoons light rum

YIELD: about 1 cup

Cream Frosting

In a heavy pan, over medium heat, caramelize ½ cup of sugar. Remove the pan from the heat for 1 minute, stir in 2 cups of light cream, and replace over heat. Turn up heat, and boil, stirring constantly, until cream is reduced and frosting is of spreading consistency. Frost cake immediately.

½ cup sugar	2 cups light cream

YIELD: about 1 cup

Napoleon Filling

Sprinkle 1 tablespoon gelatine on 2 tablespoons cold water. In the top of a double boiler, mix 3 egg yolks, ¼ cup Vanilla Sugar (see Index), and 1 tablespoon cornstarch. Gradually add 1½ cups milk, and cook, stirring constantly, until thick.

Remove from heat, add soaked gelatine, stir until dissolved, and cool completely. Whip 1½ cups heavy cream until thick with ¼ cup sugar, and fold into cooled custard.

1 tablespoon gelatine	1 tablespoon cornstarch
2 tablespoons cold water	1½ cups milk
3 egg yolks	1½ cups heavy cream
¼ cup Vanilla Sugar	¼ cup sugar

YIELD: about 4 cups

Brandied Black Cherry Sauce

Drain a 1 pound 14 ounce can of pitted black cherries (Bing cherries), reserving juice. In a saucepan, mix 1½ tablespoons cornstarch with enough of the juice to make a smooth paste. Add remaining juice, and cook, over low heat, until the juice is clear and slightly thickened. Add 2 tablespoons sugar, cook until sugar is dissolved, and remove from heat. Add the cherries, and 1 tablespoon each brandy and kirsch. Serve either slightly warmed or cold over Tsarina Rice (see Index), ice cream, plain cakes or puddings.

1 1-pound 14-ounce can of pitted black cherries	2 tablespoons sugar
	1 tablespoon brandy
1½ tablespoons cornstarch	1 tablespoon kirsch

YIELD: about 3 cups

Vanilla Sugar and Confectioners' Vanilla Sugar

To make Vanilla Sugar, slit a vanilla bean, cut into 2-inch lengths, and place in a covered jar or canister with 2 cups sugar. Allow the flavor to permeate the sugar for three or four days before using. Replenish sugar as it is used up. The flavor of the bean is retained for about six months. To make Vanilla Confectioners' Sugar, use confectioners', instead of granulated, sugar.

> 1 vanilla bean
> 2 cups granulated or confectioners' sugar

———————————•••———————————

INDEX

231

DATE DUE

FEB 23 '72 MAR 1 1991		
NOV 21 '75 DEC 1 6 1992		
APR 29 '77 SEP 1 1 1995		
NOV 25 '80		
FEB 8 1984		
MAY 2 1 1984		
NOV 2 9 1984		
JAN 4 1985		
DEC 1 9 1986